SHIPWRECKS
of the
GREAT LAKES

SHIPWRECKS
of the
GREAT LAKES

TRAGEDIES AND LEGACIES
FROM THE INLAND SEAS

ANNA LARDINOIS

Globe
Pequot

Guilford, Connecticut

Globe
Pequot

An imprint of Globe Pequot, the trade division of
The Rowman & Littlefield Publishing Group, Inc.
4501 Forbes Blvd., Ste. 200
Lanham, MD 20706
www.rowman.com

Distributed by NATIONAL BOOK NETWORK

British Library Cataloguing in Publication Information available

Library of Congress Cataloging-in-Publication Data available

ISBN 978-1-4930-5855-6 (paper : alk. paper)
ISBN 978-1-4930-5856-3 (electronic)

∞™ The paper used in this publication meets the minimum requirements of American
National Standard for Information Sciences—Permanence of Paper for Printed Library
Materials, ANSI/NISO Z39.48-1992.

With appreciation to the Wisconsin Marine Historical Society and my Milwaukee mariner friends. A special nod to my favorite swashbuckler, Corey Lardinois.

Thank you to my dear family and friends for all of their support and encouragement: The Bonesteels, The Merbeths, The Peck Row Posse, and Angie, Caroline, Jackie, Jen, Jill, and Wendy, along with countless others who have cheered me on along the way.

CONTENTS

INTRODUCTION

The Great Lakes Shipwreck Museum, located in Michigan, has determined that there have been at least six thousand shipwrecks on the Great Lakes and an estimated thirty thousand lives have been lost in those wrecks. Each of the losses is a story waiting to be told, and this collection contains a few of those stories. Shipwrecks may seem like a thing of the past, but each year these busy waterways see new maritime disasters and fatalities. This collection of stories focuses on the Great Lakes of the nineteenth and twentieth centuries, but tragedy and death are still a part of working and playing on the beautiful and dangerous Lakes.

More than Mere Lakes

Collectively, the Great Lakes are the largest body of freshwater in the world and are comprised of 21 percent of the Earth's supply of freshwater. The chain of Lakes, which spans seven hundred and fifty miles from west to east, is considered inland seas. Covering 94,250 square miles, Lakes Erie, Huron, Michigan, Ontario, and Superior are identified as seas due to their rolling waves, sustained winds, strong current, and great depths. Created by glaciers thousands of years ago, the interconnected waterway impacts the climate of the region, creating cooler summers and warmer winters, as well as increased wintertime precipitation in the area.

The Great Lakes played a key role in the development of the Midwest and were instrumental in the migration of the population westward. In the days before the railroads, the most expedient way to move people and products was on the waterways. This convenient mode of transportation, coupled with the region's rich natural resources, spawned ever-growing communities on the shores of each of the Great Lakes. Mining and forestry thrived in the area, and the steady migration of

European immigrants provided the workers needed for these new industries.

Peril on the Lakes

Tragedy is woven into the history of these important bodies of water. Capricious and deadly, the wind and waves make a potent pair that have taken lives since humans settled on the shores of these Lakes thousands of years ago. While there is a story behind every shipwreck, there are some disasters so monumental they will never be forgotten.

The Great Storm of 1913

Today, it is remembered by such colorful names as the Big Blow, the Freshwater Fury, and the White Hurricane, but when this historic storm formed over the Great Lakes, it was simply a glimpse at the awesome power of nature. Considered the deadliest and most destructive natural disaster to ever occur on the Great Lakes, the storm raged across the Lakes from November 7–10, 1913. A blizzard accompanied by hurricane-force winds took hundreds of lives and destroyed millions of dollars of property. What began as a November gale increased into a storm with 90-mile-per-hour wind gusts, thirty-five-foot waves, and whiteout snow squalls. While the storm did the greatest damage on the Lakes, shoreline communities were not spared, with cities like Cleveland reporting twenty-two inches of snowfall and snowdrifts on major thoroughfares climbing to as high as six feet.

Winds, waves, and ice punished the boats on the Lakes for sixteen hours before the storm moved north. While it is often reported that 250 sailors and crew lost their lives in the storm, some estimate the number of casualties is closer to three hundred souls. Nineteen ships were destroyed in the storm, and twelve sank, taking with them all hands on deck. Only Lake Ontario was spared from losing ships during the historic storm, and Lake Huron suffered the greatest loss with eight ships and their full crews taken by the powerful weather cycle. In the days following the storm, lakeside communities were devastated to find the bodies of drowned and frozen sailors washing up on their shores. For a time, $25 bounties were offered for each sailor recovered from the lake. Despite the financial windfall offered, the influx of dead men on their beaches left communities around the Lakes haunted by the loss of life.

In the wake of the 1913 calamity, new safety regulations were implemented that resulted in life-saving improvements to the construction of ships operating on the Lakes. Additionally, the National Weather Service (NWS) made changes to their reporting processes after the storm that resulted in safer travel on the water. Prior to the storm, the NWS only issued weather updates twice a day, which caused fast-moving storms to strike boats on the lake without notice that inclement weather was in the area. By increasing the number of weather updates, weather forecasts became more accurate and, therefore, most useful to the Great Lakes mariners.

The First Known Shipwreck

Legend has it that the first large-scale European-style ship to sail on the Great Lakes was *Le Griffon*. Built by French explorer René-Robert Cavelier, Sieur de La Salle (1643–1687), the ship was meant to sail the yet uncharted waters of the Great Lakes in hopes of discovering a Northwest Passage that would expand France's trade market into Asia. Fitted with seven cannons, she set off on her maiden voyage on August 7, 1679. Prior to *Le Griffon*, canoes were the primary vessels used on the Lakes, and the ship attracted the attention of the indigenous peoples the ship's crew of thirty-two encountered as they sailed along Lakes Erie, Huron, and Michigan.

The men traded with the local people as they sailed through the chain of Lakes. On September 18, 1679, the ship, now filled with fur pelts, began the return journey to its home port with a skeleton crew of six men. The ship was never seen again. More than three hundred years after she disappeared, rumors still swirl about the fate of the ship. Unsubstantiated tales of jealous competitors in the fur trade, a mutinous crew, and a murderous group of Native men have all been suggested as

A 1697 woodcutting of the fabled ship   **Father Louis Hennepin/Wikimedia Commons**

the cause of the disappearance of the ship, but there is no evidence to support any of these titillating stories. The cause of her sinking remains as mysterious as the location of the ship.

Today, the ship is considered the "holy grail" of shipwrecks, as it is the most storied and sought-after wreck on the Lakes. It has been declared as found an astonishing twenty-two times, but not a single discovery to date has been proven to be the elusive ship. While there are many theories about where the ship sunk, the most popular locations remain somewhere near Green Bay in Lake Michigan and near Manitoulin Island in Lake Huron.

Shipwrecks of the Great Lakes is a breezy, bite-sized look at some of the most notable disasters to occur on these celebrated and storied bodies of water. This collection identifies the wrecks of the *Eastland*, *Lady Elgin*, and the *G. P. Griffith* as the worst maritime disasters to have ever occurred on the Great Lakes, as agreed upon by most Great Lakes

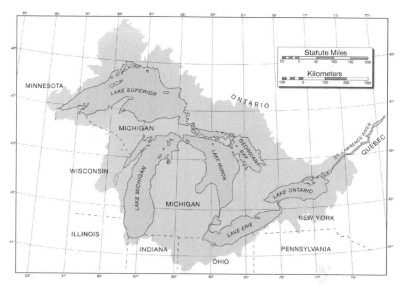

"Map of the Great Lakes with latitude, longitude, and basin outline" **NOAA Great Lakes Environmental Research Laboratory is licensed under CC BY-SA 2.0**

historians. This determination is based upon the number of lives lost in the tragedies, rather than the size of the boat or the value of the property lost in the wreck. Absent from the collection are technical details about the ships or specifics on sailing a ship; this is not a mariners' guide. Instead, prepare for swashbuckling tales of peril, loss, and survival. These stories attempt to capture the human drama and the history of these disasters that helped shape the Great Lakes region. Enjoy this collection as a great place to begin exploring the captivating true events of the inland seas that have grown into legends over the years.

LAKE ERIE

The name Erie was derived from the Iroquoian word *erielhonan*, meaning "long tail" in reference to the shape of the lake. In comparison to the other Great Lakes, Lake Erie is distinguished by being the most southerly of the chain, as well as both the warmest and the shallowest of the Lakes. The average depth of the lake is sixty-two feet, and at its greatest depth it measures at two hundred and ten feet. While Erie has a larger total area than Lake Ontario, it is smaller in volume due to its depth.

Lake Erie has been the location of many maritime disasters. According to Carrie Sowden, the archaeological director at the National Museum, there are an estimated two thousand shipwrecks beneath the waves of the lake. Only 375 of those wrecks have been located, with the oldest being the ruins of the *Lake Serpent*, which went down in 1829. The shallow water of Erie makes the wrecks easier to find on this lake than the others in the Great Lakes chain, but without the protection offered by deep, cold water, the wrecks are often in a greater state of deterioration.

Legend of the Lake Monster

The first recorded sighting of a lake serpent snaking in Lake Erie goes back to 1793. In the years that followed, the creature has been the source of fear, intrigue, speculation, and community bonding.

Newspaper accounts from the nineteenth and twentieth centuries describe a dark, slithering creature at least twenty-five feet long and a

Artist rendering of a lake sturgeon   **US Fish and Wildlife Service**

foot in diameter. Early claims describe the beast's snake-like head rising from the water, hissing at a passing boat, then lashing water with its tremendous tail. Another account, from an 1898 newspaper, describes the creature as a "fierce, ugly, coiling thing" that can travel on both land and water. Usually described with dark-colored or mottled skin, the snake-like creature has been terrifying boaters for centuries.

Some dismiss the claims that Erie harbors a lake monster, declaring that what is being seen is likely an exceptionally large sturgeon. Lake sturgeons are the oldest and largest species found in the Great Lakes. Long and bony, sturgeons have a long lifespan, with females living more than one hundred years. With their elongated, spade-like snouts, they lend themselves to serpent comparisons, yet a large sturgeon will grow to six or seven feet in length, which is significantly smaller than the reported length of the notorious creature.

Today, this creature is affectionately known as "Bessie" and has been embraced by the communities that surround the lake. A popular beer is named after the creature, as is a minor league hockey team. In 1993 there was a Cleveland-based contest that boasted a $102,000 cash prize for anyone who captured a creature from Erie that was a minimum of thirty feet long, one thousand pounds, and was a species that had yet to be identified. The prize went unclaimed. While many believe the lake is free of monsters, there is a small but determined group who are equally as certain that Bessie exists and slithers through the lake to this day.

THE INFAMOUS
PRISON SHIP:
SUCCESS (1840–1946)

The 135-foot wooden three-mast boat *Success* was built in Burma in 1840. She had a brief career as a freighter until she began her storied run as a member of the "felon fleet," the group of ships used to transport British prisoners to the Australian penal colony. It is these prison runs, and the convicts who were held aboard the ship, that have catapulted the storied ship into maritime legend. She now lies on the bottom of Lake Erie, but at one time she sailed the world, leaving tales of danger, adventure, and otherworldly occurrences in her wake.

When the ship began transporting prisoners is lost in the lore surrounding the *Success*. Some historians question the validity of the tales regarding her shipping British prisoners below the equator. It is known that the long trips from England to the Australian penal colony were miserable ones, but less clear is the role of the ship in these journeys. The often-told tales of the voyages describe men locked behind bars in dark, narrow cells below deck, where sunshine and fresh air were distant memories for the convicts. The conditions on board were filthy, and the air was foul with the stench of unwashed bodies and human waste. Rats ran rampant in the cells. As days passed on the open sea, the drinking water grew scummy, and prison rations began to rot, contributing to the misery onboard. During the journey of many months, the men remained shackled. Those whose bodies gave out on the voyage were unceremoniously

The Success *on display for tourists* **Library of Congress**

dumped overboard. Rebellion amongst the prisoners was swiftly and
brutally squelched with corporal punishments that included whippings
and torture. How often the ship was involved in this trade is not known,
with some suggesting these transports did not occur. Despite the doubts,
these stories remain tightly bound to the ship.

Not in doubt is that in 1852 the *Success* became a floating prison,
responsible for holding Australian convicts. It was the era of the Australian gold rush, and most of the ship's crew abandoned the boat in
hopes of striking it rich in mining. During this same time, the country
was being overrun with crime and did not have the capacity to house
the large number of convicts. The now crewless ship was sold to the
government and soon became one of many floating prisons anchored in
the Victoria bay. For those on both sides of the prison bars, the ship was
a perilous place. The men held in the cells were dangerous felons living
in deplorable conditions. Subjected to floggings, brandings, beatings
with cat-o'-nine-tails and other methods of punishment, brutalized
men would sometimes rebel. Perhaps the worst punishment onboard
was being placed in a "black hole," or solitary cell. Built on the sloping

side of the hull, the prisoner, chained to the wall, could neither stand up nor lie down, allowing just enough room to hunch over in the dark cage. Left for days, or even months, at a time in the black hole, some men were driven to madness in the isolation.

Among the deaths that occurred on the boat was the death of warden Owen Owens and guard John Turner in 1856, who were killed by inmate Frank McCallum, commonly known as Captain Melville. McCallum was jailed at eight years old in his native Scotland for stealing a potato pie from a food cart and transported to the penal colony. He spent the majority of his life incarcerated. In the months before the murders, McCallum was locked in a "black hole" for stabbing Owens with a sharpened spoon in retaliation for the physical punishment he received at the warden's hand. After his release from solitary confinement, the desperate prisoner tried to escape the ship, and Owens and Turner died in the process. Sentenced to death for the murders, the rakish Captain Melville was thirty-five years old when he slipped the noose around his neck and hung himself in his cell before he could be executed by the government.

Another well-known death connected to the ship is the murder of the ship's captain, John Price, who was also the inspector general of the Victoria penal establishment. In a position of ultimate authority, Price did as he pleased with the prisoners at his mercy. On March 26, 1857, a group of prisoners was taken off the ship to a work detail that required them to break stones with pickaxes and shovels. At a signal, the prisoners rushed the guards, and Price's skull was crushed by a blow to the head with a shovel. The escape was foiled, and of the thirty-two convicts who participated in the melee, seven were executed. It is likely the escape failed because prisoners always wore leg-irons that restricted their movements. The iron ball that was attached to a leg ranged in weight from seven to fifty-six pounds. If a prisoner was identified as a "rusher," or someone who attempted escape, he would be locked to a seventy-two-pound iron ball. Known as a "punishment ball," it was never removed from the convict for any reason, even hospital visits, and some prisoners were buried with the ball still riveted to their legs.

The murders sparked investigations of the onboard conditions on the ships. These studies helped highlight the cruelty that occurred on the ships. By 1885, Australia, having banned the floating prisons, ordered all of the prison hulks destroyed. Somehow, the *Success* eluded the destruction of the ships, and within five years the ship that had seen so much misery began its new identity as a tourist attraction.

The salacious news stories about the horrors of the prison boats created interest in the vessel, and the new owner was eager to capitalize on the dark curiosity of customers. After towing the boat to the Sydney Harbor, he outfitted the ship with wax models of prisoners and put the mannequins in the cells to recreate scenes from the ship's horrible past. Along with some of the real implements of torture used on board, the theatrical owner added some historically inaccurate implements as well, including an iron maiden, in a quest to enthrall visitors. No circus is complete without a ringmaster, so former prisoner Harry Power was hired to give tours of the notorious boat. An elderly man by the time he worked on the boat where he was once imprisoned, his age did nothing to diminish his showmanship.

Powers, birth name Harry Johnstone, served fourteen years aboard the ship in cell twenty-four for shooting a police trooper. A notorious bushranger, he is believed to have been a part of the legendary criminal Ned Kelly's gang. Power also was connected to the convicted murderer "Mad" Dan Morgan, who too served time on the *Success*. It is suspected Powers and Morgan committed more than one murder together.

Once the ship was opened to the public, stories began to circulate that the ship was haunted by those prisoners who suffered aboard the *Success*. Reports from employees and visitors of the sound of disembodied moaning and shrieks of pain coming from below deck were common. There were claims that ghostly arms would reach out from between the bars of a cell, sometimes touching a person who stepped too close to the locked cages. Whether part of his act, or as a result of true fear, Powers refused to go near the cell that held him for so many years, claiming that an unsettling spirit lurked in the dank hole. It is

Torture irons used on prisoners displayed aboard the Success   **Library of Congress**

said employees refused to go below deck in the evenings due to the supernatural phenomena, a refusal which became a source of difficulty when the boat got a crew and began to sail around the world to show off the macabre relic.

Once Australians tired of the ship, it set sail for London in 1895, where it titillated tourists until it was purchased by an enterprising man named John Scott. In 1912, Scott sailed the ship to Boston and began a tour of the United States. With her grisly tales and her eerie reputation, the *Success* brought in visitors wherever she was docked. She was sailed through the Panama Canal so she could be on exhibit at the 1916 World's Fair in San Francisco. In 1923, she arrived on the Great Lakes, where she was a big hit in both Chicago and Cleveland. In 1933, she appeared at the Chicago World's Fair. She continued to change hands as she traveled, and each year she became more weatherworn. The now shabby boat leaked, and its aging displays were not able to draw crowds like she did in the past. Men who knew how to sail the three-mast schooner had long ago stopped working the waters, so unable to find sailors to man the ship, she was towed from port to port.

The artifact of an earlier time limped along until 1943 when she sank during a storm on Lake Erie. She remained under the waves for a year until she was bought by a man who thought she could still bring in the crowds. They pumped the hull of the submerged boat and raised her, but she got stuck in a sandbar about a half mile from shore. Unable to move the newly raised ship, the owner decided to leave her there for a season; but a season became many seasons, and while she waited she was relentlessly pounded by waves, cracked by ice, and even looted by vandals who stripped her of her valuables. Soon, the ship that had once been the stuff of nightmares was considered nothing more than what the US Coast Guard called a "hazard to navigation." They ordered the owner to move the ship off the sandbar and out of the way of passing boats.

Ravaged and largely worthless, the *Success* had one more opportunity to put on a show. On the evening of July 4, 1946, those who gathered to the lakefront near Port Clinton, Ohio, to see the annual fireworks display witnessed the *Success*' grand finale: the boat went up in flames. No one knows who set the fire that destroyed the ship, yet rumors persist that the fire was no accident, with some claiming the boat's owner set the fire to free himself from the expense of moving the scrapped boat. Whoever the arsonist was, it is fitting that the ship, once celebrated for its connection to criminals, met its end at the hand of one.

A RARE JUNE GALE: *MARGARET OLWILL* (1887–1899)

Clinging to floating pieces of what was the cabin house of the ship, Duncan and George tried desperately to keep their heads above the water. Wave after wave crashed over them, and the wind howled fiercely across the lake, yet they battled to hang on to the splintered wood. They had been in the water for four hours and were exhausted from the struggle to stay above the waves and numb from the cold water. Despite their pain and fear, as the sun rose, they felt a renewed hope that the daylight would allow a passing ship to spot the desperate men and reach them before it was too late.

At just after five in the morning, the SS *State of Ohio* came across a field of wreckage floating in the water. A powerful gale bellowed throughout the night, and the captain suspected he may have come across a ship that was wrecked in the storm that was still raging. He scanned the area, searching for survivors. After sailing for an hour, Captain Willoughby spotted the storm-ravaged cabin house tossing about in the water. He looked closer and spotted the men struggling to hold on to the ship's wreckage. The storm was too powerful to send any of his crew out in a lifeboat to rescue the men, and he knew the desperate-looking men needed help soon, before they slipped beneath the water for a final time. With few options, the crew tossed lifelines to the men, which they needed to catch and wrap around themselves so they could

The Margaret Olwill *in her final months on Lake Erie* **WikiCommons**

be pulled onto the boat. Wasting no time, the *Ohio* began tossing lines to the men.

George Heffron watched the lifeline fly through the air and land time and again just out of his reach. The crew of the *Ohio* was on their deck, shouting words of encouragement to the man, and after many tries, the rope finally came near enough to him that he was able to grab it. With the rope in his hand, he struggled to wrap it around his waist. Overcome by the effort to put on the lifeline, the weakened man slipped beneath the waves one final time. The crew of the *Ohio* looked on in horror as he disappeared into the murky deep. Determined not to lose Duncan Coyle, the crew did all they could to encourage the man to quickly fasten the line around his waist. Using the last of his strength, Duncan secured himself to the lifeline, and the men of the *Ohio* dragged him aboard. Willoughby would later describe Coyle as "more dead than alive" when he was pulled onto the deck. Believing Coyle to be the sole survivor, the *Ohio* sailed on to her destination.

In the distance, three other crewmen clung to wreckage from the sunken ship. Battling the waves, they watched the *Ohio* rescue Coyle.

Their shouts for help were lost in the howling wind, and they could do nothing to get the attention of the *Ohio* crew. The men continued to fight for their lives in the storm as the *Ohio* sailed away from them. Before the men lost hope, the SS *Sacramento* sailed by the wreckage field and noticed the stranded men. The 308-foot ship had difficulty maneuvering close enough to the men to rescue them. *Cascade*, a passing tug, noticed the *Sacramento* was moving strangely in the water. Thinking the boat was in trouble, the *Cascade* sailed closer to the *Sacramento*. Once it was clear the steamer was attempting to save the shipwrecked sailors, the *Cascade* aided the effort, and all three men were taken from Erie alive.

Once the men regained strength, they were able to tell the story of their ordeal. They set sail from the quarry on Kelley Island on the *Margaret Olwill*, June 28, 1899, at six in the evening. The 176-foot, three-mast wooden screw steamer was bound for Cleveland with a load of limestone. Her hold was filled to capacity with three hundred tons of rock, and her open decks were piled high with another six hundred tons of rock. The summer weather had been mild, and Captain John Brown brought his wife, Lizzie, her friend, and the Brown's young son, Blanchard, on the short run. All thirteen aboard expected a pleasant run on a calm lake.

As the sun set, the winds increased, and by ten in the evening, the small freighter was up against 50-mile-an-hour winds. The heavily laden ship twisted in the waves, and she began to crack along her seams. The hold was filling with the water pouring in from the many fractures, and the ship began to list dangerously. By two in the morning, Captain Brown decided that the *Margaret Olwill* could not sustain the powerful gale and turned the ship to seek safe harbor. As the ship was making the turn, she lost her steering. Unable to complete the turn, the ship was hit broadside by a powerful wave. Aware the ship was in danger, the captain called for everyone aboard to board the lifeboat. This order came too late; before the evacuation could begin, she was hit by another mighty wave and capsized. The cabin house ripped free from the *Olwill* as she turned and floated away as the rest of the ship sunk to the

Laborers on Kelley Island **Rutherford B. Hayes Presidential Center OhioLINK Digital Resource Commons**

bottom of the churning lake. A few lucky sailors managed to grab onto the floating wreckage as the ship rolled, saving themselves. The Brown family and their guest were not among those who fled before the ship sank. In total, nine people aboard drowned in the rare summer gale.

In the days that followed, Erie began to give up some of the bodies of those lost on the *Olwill*. Father and son were recovered together on July 14, and Mrs. Brown's friend was found by a farmer later in the month. As the corpses were pulled from the lake, there was a need to blame someone for this tragedy. The captain's brother, also a captain on the Great Lakes, believed the deaths were the fault of the boat owners, who pressured captains to sail overloaded boats in inclement weather, always putting profits above the safety of those who manned their boats. Others blamed the fickle weather, claiming no one could have predicted a powerful, sustained storm in the summer, particularly during a season that had been notably mild. There were a few who mentioned that perhaps this wreck might be connected to the spirits of angry miners who lost their lives in the quarry on Kelley Island. Legend has it that a group of miners who drowned in an excavation accident in the quarry remain as vengeful spirits on the island. Some believe those who lost their lives in the pursuit of the profitable rocks have a hand in the sinking of ships that carry the rocks from the island. The tales of the cursed cargo persist, and many other boats are part of the folklore; after all, the *Margaret Olwill* was far from the only ship loaded with rock from the island that met the bottom of Lake Erie.

The final resting place of the *Margaret Olwill* and those trapped aboard when she sank remained a mystery until 2017, when she was rediscovered by divers near Lorain, Ohio. She lies under the waves and is covered in silt, so it is not known if any of the missing are still inside the wooden steamer.

A CENTURY-LONG SAGA: *ATLANTIC* (1849–1852)

The wreck of the *Atlantic*, with its large number of fatalities, is rated the fifth-worst disaster to ever occur on the Great Lakes. Many of the dead, mostly nameless recent immigrants who boarded the paddle steamer with their hearts full of hope as they traveled to their new homes, still lie beneath Lake Erie's waves. It took 144 years before those who died aboard the *Atlantic* were able to truly rest in peace. Their journey began on a summer night in 1852 and finally came to an end in a Canadian courtroom in 1996.

In her day, the *Atlantic* was quite a ship; she was bigger and faster than most of the other ships sailing on the Great Lakes at the time. The passenger ship could hold three hundred guests and boasted eighty-five staterooms outfitted in mahogany and trimmed with gleaming gold gilt. For ten dollars, a passenger could enjoy a luxurious cabin, dine at marble-topped tables, and dance in the lounge. In contrast, a dollar ticket would get the holder entry to the ship and little else. These ticketholders often settled in on hurricane decks and created makeshift beds on top of their suitcases. The journey was not comfortable, but it was fast.

On August 19, 1852, the *Atlantic*, captained by J. Byron Pett(e)y, left Buffalo for Detroit, with stops at destinations in between. Operating at top speeds, she could make that journey in under seventeen hours.

Artist rendering of the Atlantic *(1849–1852)* **Lake Erie's Yesterdays, OhioLINK Digital Resource Commons**

Her cabins were full, and both steerage and decks were approaching full capacity with approximately 250 passengers onboard. She stopped in Erie, Pennsylvania, and brought aboard many more passengers, primarily Norwegian immigrants making their way to farmland in the Midwest. The boat was now filled beyond capacity, with an estimated five to six hundred passengers aboard. The *Atlantic* had to turn away at least seventy people in Erie, as the boat could not handle any additional passengers. The unlucky group left on the dock in disappointment but would soon be thankful for this stroke of bad luck.

Passengers sat anywhere there was room as the boat sailed into open waters. It was a warm, still night on the lake. Hazy and moonless, the ship's running lights glowed in the fog as she made her way west. Also sailing that night was the propeller steamer *Ogdensburg*, who was traveling from Cleveland to New York. In the early morning hours, the *Ogdensburg*'s first mate spotted the *Atlantic* in the distance. Based on the position of the two boats and their estimated speeds, the man judged the *Ogdensburg* would pass about a half mile ahead of the *Atlantic*, so *Ogdensburg* kept her course. Unexpectedly, the *Atlantic* changed its course, and a collision was imminent. The first mate immediately signaled the *Ogdensburg*'s engine room to reverse its engines and commanded the wheelman to make a hard portside turn. The ship's whistle was out of order, so the first mate sped to the hurricane deck, calling out to the *Atlantic* to make a starboard turn. His frantic cries were unheard.

Only two minutes passed between the first mate's orders to change course and the bow of his ship striking the *Atlantic* midship on her portside. Around two-thirty in the morning, passengers on the *Atlantic* were jolted awake from the force of the collision. The crew of the *Atlantic* quickly decided to race full speed ahead for the Long Point shore, an estimated four miles in the distance, in an effort to beach the boat and save all those aboard. The sounds of splintering wood filled the air, but the engines continued to hum, reassuring all onboard that the *Atlantic* was sound.

As the *Atlantic* steamed forward, the crew of the *Ogdensburg* also believed the ship was not damaged. Captain Richardson of the *Ogdensburg* awoke when the engines were put in reverse and evaluated the damage done to his ship's bow as the *Atlantic* sailed away. The damage to the bow was significant, and Richardson was unconvinced that the *Atlantic*, struck hard in the middle of the ship, would not also be seriously damaged. The *Ogdensburg* traveled two miles from the collision before the captain ordered the crew to turn the boat around and follow the *Atlantic* to ensure its safety.

Richardson was correct; the *Atlantic* had been badly damaged in the collision, but most aboard the ship did not know they were in trouble. The ship was hit broadside and had a breach below her waterline. As the engines moved forward at full throttle, torrents of water flooded the lower decks. Passengers in the forward below decks likely drowned in their beds in the moments after the collision. The rushing water also flooded the engines, and the boat lost power about a half mile from the collision. Despite the dire situation, crew did not wake the sleeping passengers and did not begin to ring the alarm bell until the engines stopped and it was clear the ship was sinking.

Frightened, pajama-clad passengers, many of whom did not speak English, filled the decks. Soon the boat began to list notably to the portside. Receiving no direction from the crew, passengers began to jump into the dark water to avoid going down with the ship. Rather than life preservers, the ship had stools fitted with tin pans beneath the seat to make them buoyant and that were meant to be used as a flotation device. Some threw the stools into the water first, then attempted to jump onto them, a move that was often unsuccessful. Many who took their chances in the water that night drowned.

As the desperate jumped into Erie's still, black water, the ship's lifeboats were lowered. With just three boats and upwards of five hundred passengers, there were few opportunities to flee the ship. The first lifeboat was clumsily lowered, causing the boat to capsize, dumping all aboard into the water except for the ship's captain, Petty. The two other lifeboats were also largely filled with crew. Before long, the ship's smokestacks gave way, crashing onto the deck and collapsing on a group of passengers, some of whom were fatally injured by the falling pipes. Soon, the bow and midsection of the *Atlantic* sunk below the waterline. An air bubble trapped inside the ship caused the stern of the ship to rise out of the water, giving those still alive another chance to outrun the water that was consuming the boat.

In the midst of the chaos, passengers noticed boat lights coming their way. It was the *Ogdensburg* sailing toward the *Atlantic*. As the ship approached, the crew heard desperate screams piercing the fog-filled night and panicked pleas for rescue. Once they were close enough to peer through the fog, the crew of the *Ogdensburg* was stunned by what they saw. The water was teeming with people, both living and dead, and there were still hundreds clinging to the stern side of the half-sunken ship. Richardson and his crew acted quickly, maneuvering the *Ogdensburg* alongside the foundering *Atlantic* so the trapped passengers could climb from one ship to the other. While this was happening, the crew was busy pulling survivors from the water. Richardson and his crew heroically saved the lives of hundreds that night, yet before the sun rose

Artist rendering of the collision between the Atlantic *and the* Ogdensburg **Lake Erie's Yesterdays, OhioLINK Digital Resource Commons**

on August 20, 1852, the *Atlantic* was at the bottom of Lake Erie and hundreds of lives were lost.

The sinking of the *Atlantic* is considered to be the fifth-greatest loss of life on the Great Lakes; however, the exact number of people who died that night will never be known. The ship's passenger list was lost, so it is uncertain how many people were aboard that night. Many of those lost were recent immigrants who were en route to their new communities. No one in the United States knew who they were, or even their names. For their loved ones in their home countries, the travelers simply vanished, never to be heard from again. It is commonly believed between 130 and 300 people died that night, with many citing 250 deaths as the most accurate estimate of the number of fatalities.

The *Ogdensburg* dropped most of the survivors off at the same Erie pier where they boarded the *Atlantic* just hours earlier. The wet, exhausted survivors were now penniless and without even basic clothing, as most were in their pajamas when the accident occurred. Everything many of them owned in the world sunk with the ship. The city of Erie, as well as other cities along the route, rallied around the survivors, offering them hotel rooms, free telegram transmission, clothing, and food. The State Line Railroad offered free transport to the final destinations of the stranded passengers, and the *Sultana* offered passage to those who were ready to risk another boat ride on the lake. The survivors acknowledged the kindness they received from the community, as well as their deep appreciation to Captain Richardson and the crew of the *Ogdensburg* for their rescue in a series of public statements.

While grateful for the help they received, the survivors of the *Atlantic* were angry and quickly organized and drafted resolutions denouncing the owners of the *Atlantic* and her derelict crew. They lambasted Captain Petty for his lack of leadership and admonished the crew for deserting the sinking vessel. They declared the decision to speed forward, rather than stop after the collision where they could have immediately evacuated to the *Ogdensburg*, as a primary cause for the large loss of life. There was heavy criticism for the stools that were meant to be used as life preservers. The group indicated that many did not float, and the ones that did easily tipped over in the water. One passenger likened the stools to "manslaughter." The group had praise for one member of the *Atlantic* crew: the clerk Mr. Givon. He was cited as a calming presence during the crisis and was the last man off the sinking ship. Their grievances were many but seemingly well justified, and newspapers around the country published the open letters of complaint, often alongside updated news of the sinking.

Survivors from the wreck begged the *Atlantic*'s owner to send a boat to the site of the sinking to immediately retrieve the bodies of the dead. They were concerned that if the bodies washed ashore, they would be left stripped and looted and, therefore, unidentifiable. At that time, it was common practice for immigrants to sew valuables into their clothing and to keep large sums of money on their person, making the corpses attractive targets for thieves. It took several days for the owners to comply and send a boat to remove the bodies from the lake.

In the days that followed, analysis of the accident revealed why the tragedy occurred. It was determined that the collision was caused by the hazy conditions, coupled with both ships misjudging the distance between the two vessels. The high death toll of the accident was largely blamed on the captain and crew of the sunken ship. The lack of lifeboats was a definite factor in the number of deaths that night, as was the failure of the crew to wake the passengers after the collision. In the final analysis, it was concluded that the lack of leadership in the crisis, highlighted by the fact the captain and much of the crew abandoned the ship as she went down, was the key cause for the high death toll. The fight to assign blame for the tragedy raged for years and was finally decided by the US Supreme Court in 1859, who found both boats equally responsible for the collision.

Along with the lives of hundreds and the worldly possessions of many, the ship went down with a stash of US mail from Buffalo, bound for Detroit, and a safe owned by American Express that contained cash, gold, and stock certificates. American Express wanted the contents of the safe returned, so they hired Canadian-born diver John Green to retrieve the safe. To make the 150-foot dive, Green donned a rubber diving suit with a copper helmet with a glass porthole and was attached by rubber hose to a breathing apparatus that required four to six men to run the machine while he was underwater. In his first attempt in the weeks that followed the accident, Green made it 105 feet below the water but had to abandon the dive when it appeared his air hoses might burst. His second dive was the deepest that anyone had made on the Great Lakes at that time but was marred by the tangling of his lifelines. As fall, and its stormy weather, approached, diving was halted for the remainder of the season. Still eager to reclaim their money, the company then hired a company to raise the ship, but the effort was unsuccessful. They tried their luck again with Green the following year, and he was finally able to reach the stateroom on the wreck where the safe was kept but found he needed a hook to retrieve it. Days later, he made the dive again, certain he would finally collect the safe and a handsome payment for his efforts, but the dive needed to be abandoned when Green developed decompression sickness during the dive. The ailment, commonly referred to as "the bends," results from a build-up of nitrogen bubbles in the body. Green was left with temporarily paralyzed lower extremities and would not attempt to retrieve the safe again until the following year.

When Green made his next attempt, he was stunned. The safe was gone! Rival diver Elliot Harrington had been keeping an eye on Green's progress and collected the safe himself. After some legal wrangling, in 1856, American Express got their safe, and Harrington received $7,000 in excavation fees, leaving Green sorely disappointed. It would not be the last time divers would battle over what remained on the ship.

The 267-foot passenger steamer with the three-storm paddle wheel continued to intrigue people long after she sank. In 1984, Canadian diver Michael Fletcher began exploring the wreck. Devoted to maritime archeology, Fletcher spent his time recording what he discovered aboard the still largely intact ship. Considering it a historical time capsule, he wanted the wreck to remain undisturbed and kept its whereabouts a secret. In 1991, a California treasure hunting company discovered Fletcher's dive markers and boarded the wreck, removing from it a number of artifacts. The company attempted to claim ownership of the boat by paying the back taxes owed on the sunken vessel and having a California court declare the company the owner of the wreck.

The wreck, which is also the final resting place of countless bodies lost that summer night in 1852, is on the Canadian side of the lake. Canadian interests claimed that the wreck belonged to Canada, while the Californian company argued the boat was owned by a US company and carried both US passengers and US mail, making it a concern of the United States. The debate, which went on for years, was finally decided in a Canadian court at the close of 1996. It was determined that the ship belonged to the Ontario government and must remain undisturbed. The precise location of the *Atlantic* is known to few to protect the ship and its contents from looting.

With that ruling, at last, those who started the journey to start a new life more than a century ago were finally able to rest in peace. Still nameless, but not forgotten, their watery grave will no longer be disturbed.

ERIE'S GREATEST TRAGEDY: *G. P. GRIFFITH* (1849–1850)

I t was an idyllic June night as the *G. P. Griffith* glided along Lake Erie's dark water. The warm air and calm waves had lulled most of the paddle steamboat's estimated three hundred passengers into a deep slumber, with many of them choosing to make their beds on the hurricane deck rather than in the cramped and stuffy quarters below deck for which they had paid. Most were on the last leg of journeys that had begun in Germany, Norway, or the British Isles, and they were on their way to Cleveland, Toledo, Chicago, or any one of the smaller towns in between the sidewheeler would stop in on this voyage. As the water gently lapped against the sides of the wooden ship, its passengers likely dreamed of the new life they were about to begin in the United States. These adventurous dreamers, and the twenty-five crew members onboard, would soon become unwitting participants in American maritime history as the *Griffith* sailed into the night.

Spirits were high when the ship left the Buffalo port on June 16, 1850. Captain C. C. Roby brought his wife Amelia, twelve-year-old daughter Abby, and mother-in-law on the voyage, eager to treat the beloved trio to a pleasure cruise through the Lakes. As day passed into night, Roby settled his family into the captain's quarters, and the ship's passengers and much of the crew turned in for what they anticipated would be a restful night on calm waters.

At three in the morning, wheelsman Richard Mann noticed sparks on the cabin roof, near the boat's smokestack. Mann alerted the first mate, William Evens, of the smoldering embers, and shortly, the deckhands began a bucket brigade to extinguish the flames that had begun flickering on the wooden roof of the cabin. Bucket after bucket of water was tossed upon the growing fire to no avail, and soon the blaze raged out of control. The fire alarm was sounded, and shouts of "feuer" and "brann" joined the cries of "fire" as the passengers were notified of the danger.

Roused from sleep, confused families scrambled from their steerage quarters below deck, along the dark, narrow passageways that would lead them to safety. Panic spread as passengers fled from the flames; a few stumbled in the rush toward safety and were trampled beneath the feet of those seeking an escape. Many of the immigrant families were carrying all of their possessions onboard, and despite the growing danger, some were hesitant to abandon their valuables. Those who had not already sewn gold and jewelry into the seams of their clothing strapped on their money belts and filled their pockets with all they could carry. Weighted down with all they managed to stash on their bodies, these men and women maneuvered the now smoke-filled passageways and heaved themselves onto the deck of the ship.

As the passengers clamored to avoid the rapidly growing fire, Captain Roby calculated the ship was between two and three miles from the shore. Knowing he had to act fast, he decided he would beach the ship, which would allow passengers to escape from the fiery vessel into the shallow water, and then walk to the safety of the shore. The ship sailed at full speed toward the beach, which only fanned the flames of the fire, and the blaze quickly spread to the aft. The ship was moving too fast to lower its smoldering lifeboats, gambling that the boat would reach the shore before the ship became fully engulfed in flames. As the *Griffith* moved toward the beach, the winds coming off the shore further fed the ravenous flames. To the horror of all aboard, the hurricane deck, now packed with passengers, began to burn. There was now nowhere left for those onboard to run, and the fire surrounded them.

A depiction of the steamship G. P. Griffith *burning in 1850 as found in* Lloyd's Steamboat Directory and Disasters on the Western Waters **James T. Lloyd, 1856, WikiCommons**

Screams of anguish from those caught in cabins and burned alive filled the night as the ship sped toward shore. The acrid smell of burnt hair and flesh stung the nostrils of those onboard. On deck, men beat the flames from long beards and overcoats, and mothers held their children to their breasts, wrapping them inside their shawls in a desperate bid to protect their offspring from the choking smoke and flames. In the midst of the chaos, there was a sudden, violent lurch, and then the *Griffith* came to a halt. In the darkness, it was thought the ship had made it to shore and that passengers and crew could walk from the fire-ravaged ship to the safety of the beach. The promise of a rescue was quickly snatched from their grasp as they realized they had run aground on a sandbar, not the beach, and were an estimated half mile from shore in water more than eight feet deep. The ship could not free itself from the sandbar and was now fully ablaze. There was nothing left to be done but to jump into the deep, dark water and try to survive.

The first few passengers to flee the ship were caught in the ship's rotating paddle wheel. Those still onboard witnessed the paddle wheel, with a thirty-one-foot diameter and still spinning at full speed, suck the

jumpers into its rotation. The paddles beat the bodies of the jumpers, then forced them under the water, as one survivor recalled, "some
bloodied bodies were carried up on the paddles to the top of the arc
only to be thrown ruthlessly back into the lake." Despite the horrific
scene, the fire continued to sweep through the ship so passengers were
forced to jump into the lake with the hope they could avoid the paddle
wheel or else burn to death.

The lifeboats were lost to the flames, and no flotation devices were
distributed to the passengers, as they planned to run the ship into
shallow water. Most onboard could not swim and struggled in the water
before disappearing beneath the waves. Men wearing money belts filled
with the gold, silver, and coins saved over years and women with treasures sewn into the hems of their dresses were weighed down by their
valuables and drowned. In the panic to stay above the surface of the
water, desperate people clung to those near them, inadvertently pulling
them down with them to the bottom of the lake. Those who could swim
were able to dive away from the boat and its perils, but they soon discovered they were too far from shore to make it to shallow water before
they were overcome with exhaustion and they, too, drowned. As this
scene unfolded, Captain Roby prepared his family to flee the burning
ship. A survivor recalled what Captain Roby said to them:

> "Dear wife, prepare to meet the worst." Then clasping her in
> his arms convulsively, and kissing her, as quick as thought he
> whirled her over the railing and into the Lake. He then seized
> his wife's mother and threw her overboard, then his little daugh-
> ter, and closed the sad scene by jumping after them, all to take
> their chances of life, which were against them.

As the fire raged on, its brilliant glow drew nearby residents to the
lakeshore. The orange flames illuminated the dark water, revealing the
lifeless bodies of the drowned bobbing in the waves. Soon, the dead
began to wash up on shore to join those who gathered on the beach to
watch the ship burn. Along with the corpses, travel trunks, paperwork

from the ship, and the cherished possessions of the travelers and crew were carried by the waves onto the sandy shore. As the ship smoldered in the distance, rescue boats made their way toward the disaster, but they quickly discovered theirs would largely be a recovery mission. Erie was clear and placid that morning, allowing the men to see the hundreds of bodies that sunk to the bottom of the lake. As they searched the water, they found the lifeless bodies of mothers protectively clutching their dead children to their breasts and entire families still clinging to each other in death, their pleas for help forever silenced. Discovered among the dead were the bodies of Captain Roby and his wife, locked in an eternal embrace. Nearby, the bodies of their daughter and her grandmother were also recovered from the lake. Despite the overwhelming number of corpses in the water, there was evidence that many died a fiery death. James Stacy, a member of the recovery crew, reported that the deck of the *Griffith* was "covered in the bones of the burned." Of the 326 passengers and crew who left Buffalo on June 16, 1850, only forty people survived the wreck that remains Lake Erie's most deadly maritime disaster. Every child aboard the ship was either burned to death or drowned, and only one woman, the ship barber's wife, who entered the water with the captain's family, survived the tragedy.

All that morning, the bodies of the drowned and the salvageable remains of the burnt were taken to the shore. Soon, the number of bodies overwhelmed the space, and the crew began stacking the corpses as if they were logs. Survivor Dr. William Maronehy of Wachita, Louisiana, remembers those handling the hundreds of corpses on the beach placed leafy branches over the faces of the dead as a sign of respect. Of the estimated 286 who perished on the *Griffith*, ninety-seven of the bodies that were recovered could not be identified. As the hot June sun beat down on the growing pile of unidentified bodies, a trench was quickly dug for a mass burial. Laid to rest in an unmarked grave on the shore of Lake Erie were forty-seven men, twenty-four women, and twenty-five children, all who remain nameless to this day.

In fifty years' time, many in the area had forgotten the tragedy of the *Griffith*, and the lake had long ago washed away any evidence that the mass grave had ever been dug on Lake Erie's scenic shore. So pictur-esque was the location that from 1900 into the 1920s it was the spot of the Willoughbeach Amusement Park. Throngs of tourists seeking entertainment flocked to the grounds, and when they sat down to rest at the picnic tables near the shore, they sat directly above the mass grave of those lost in the tragic wreck. The patrons may not have known they dined above the bones of the dead, but employees of the park certainly did, as it was part of their job to dispose of the human bones that poked through the surface of the eroded soil. Eventually, the gravesite, and whatever remains were not destroyed by the park workers, were reclaimed by the lake, its ceaseless waves washing away all traces of those unfortunate casualties of Erie's deadliest night.

THE CALL OF THE WHISTLE: SS *CLARION* (1881–1909)

The winds were wild the night of December 8, 1909. The heavy seas crashed over the deck of the 240-foot wooden steamer. They sailed the 1,700-ton freighter loaded with coal along the southeast shoal of Point Pelee, Ontario through heavy sheets of snow. The dense fog hung all around them, freezing to the faces of the men, and ice clung to the lines of the ship as the men fought through the roughest storm of the season. The ship's aged engineer, Alfred Welch, and the first mate, Jim Thompson, exchanged glances. They both smelled it, the distinct odor of wood smoke. Knowing the ship's coal-fired boiler wasn't the source of the scent, Thompson, with a fire extinguisher in hand, went below deck to investigate the smell at seven in the evening. It was the last time Welch would see the first mate alive.

Moments after Thompson descended the stairs, the ship's lights went out, leaving the sailors in the blackness of the stormy night. Thick, sooty smoke filled the ship's passageways. Minutes ago, the *Clarion* was fighting to stay above the waves in the storm, and now the ship was on fire. The storm's gale-force winds fed the hungry flames, and the fire quickly moved through the wooden ship. Welch rushed to find Thompson, only to discover him just feet from where they parted, dead in the passageway, likely overcome by smoke inhalation. Welch left the crumpled body of the man on the floor and rushed to notify the ship's captain.

Captain E. J. Bell thought he could save the crew by running the ship aground in the shoals, but the fire was spreading too quickly for them to do anything other than flee the ship. The captain and twelve of the forward crew entered the ship's metal lifeboat and set off toward the Point Pelee lifesaving station, less than a mile away from where the storm-tossed *Clarion* was being ravaged by flames. The group left quickly, bringing nothing with them but the clothes on their backs, thinking neither food nor supplies would be needed for the short journey. The seven men who remained on the boat continued to send distress signals in hopes of being rescued by the Point Pelee lighthouse keeper, Captain Grubbs, but the heavy snowfall made it impossible for their signals to be seen. Despite the thick fog, men aboard waved lanterns, hopeful the light would bring aid to the ship. With the inferno raging below him, Welch gripped the rungs of the ship's smokestack ladder, manually operating the ship's whistle, sending a distress signal without pause in hopes someone would hear their cries for help.

The *Clarion*'s wooden yawl was lowered into the stormy waters so the remaining seven men could flee the ship. The heavy waves pounded the small boat, and she was filled with water before the men were able to board the yawl. Joe McCauley began to bale the yawl when the heavy seas capsized the boat, and McCauley was pulled beneath the waves, never to resurface. The boat was lost, and the men, now six in number, had just lost their only way off the flame-ravaged *Clarion*. Their only chance for survival was a rescue, but the storm made it impossible for them to know if anyone could receive their calls for help. Minutes turned to hours as the six men watched the fire chew through the ship. Welch kept up his tireless signaling on the whistle, and the men neared ever closer to the edge of the ship in an effort to evade the growing fire.

Fortunately, the nearby steamer *H. P. Bope*, the first freighter on the Great Lakes to have wireless service onboard, spotted the fire through the blizzard and notified the ports a ship was ablaze. The *Josiah G. Munro* heard the *Bope*'s call for aid and sailed out to the southeastern

The SS Clarion *was a cargo ship that caught fire on Lake Erie on December 8, 1909, during a gale.* **Lake Erie's Yesterdays OhioLINK Digital Resource Commons**

shoal of Point Pelee. The *Bope* had not specified the *Clarion*'s location, so the 530-foot *Munro* crept along the dangerous shoal hoping to see something emerge from the dense fog. At last, the *Munro* caught a glimpse of the fiery boat, drifting in the waves, as it lost control of its steering in the blaze. The boat attempted to reach the *Clarion* but ran aground in the dangerous shoals. Stuck on the jagged stones, the *Munro* could do nothing other than helplessly watch on as the boat drifted away. The six stranded men, again, watched their opportunity to flee the burning ship disappear before them.

Four hours after the storm tossed the yawl away from the *Clarion*, salvation arrived in the form of Captain Anderson and the SS *Leonard C. Hanna*. With the storm still raging, Anderson sailed over to the flaming vessel to offer his aid. He could see the men needed help quickly or they would be consumed by the flames. Pounding waves and howling winds continued, making it too dangerous to send a lifeboat to the trapped sailors. Nearly snow blind, Anderson managed a daring rescue. He steered the 504-foot ship near the burning boat. He was close, but he knew he would need to be much closer to the ship in order to reach the men. He circled the ship three times, each time getting ever closer to the boat, until she finally was close enough for the stranded men to leap from the flaming *Clarion* onto the *Hanna*.

Five men leapt between the ships before the *Clarion* had to pull away. The intrepid Welch was alone on the deck. As flames poked through the floorboards and smoke stung his eyes, he watched the *Hanna* circle back around the boat. He hoped Anderson could manage the daring feat once again. With breathless anticipation, Welch watched for a half an hour as the *Hanna* again circled nearer until the ships were no more than a foot apart, and he leapt over the rails of both ships, landing safely on the deck on the *Hanna*.

Reunited and finally safe, the men were taken to Cleveland, where they were treated for exhaustion and exposure, and then they were quickly whisked off by train to Buffalo to meet with the boat's owners. Once in the offices of Anchor Line, the six survivors raged against the captain of the *Bope*, claiming he could have saved the entire crew of the failing ship had he stopped for them rather than simply call for help. An angry sailor stated, "like brutal cowards they kept right along on their course and left us to die like rats in a trap." The captain denied the claims, explaining the intensity of the storm, coupled with the speed at which the 540-foot *Munro* traveled, made it impossible for them to stop and help the *Clarion*. In the end, it was determined that the survivors' claims were the result of "exhaustion and overwrought emotions." It was during this time that the search for the missing thirteen men in the metal lifeboat was called off, and the sailors were presumed dead.

The storm that night was a brutal one, and by the time it passed over Lake Erie, four boats and fifty-nine sailors lay beneath the waves. Only two of the fifteen men who died on the *Clarion* were ever recovered. McCauley was found on April 6, 1910, in the Niagara River, near Buffalo. What happened to the thirteen men who launched the lifeboat away from the flaming ship and into the storm will never be known, but the body of the *Clarion*'s captain, Bell, who was aboard the lifeboat, was found by fishermen in Ontario on October 10, 1910. All doubt about the body's identity was removed when a letter written by Bell's wife was found in the pocket of the corpse clad in a captain's uniform. It was unclear from the body whether the men capsized during the storm or succumbed to its deadly cold. The remaining men lie in watery graves at the bottom of Lake Erie, the story of their final moments forever untold.

LAKE HURON

Lake Huron is the fifth-largest freshwater lake in the world. It ranks as the second largest of the Great Lakes in surface area and the third largest by volume. Measuring 206 miles across with a width of 183 miles, the lake has a surface area of 23,000 square miles. Huron's average depth is 195 feet and is 750 at its deepest. Originally called "La Mer Donce," or "Freshwater Sea," by the French, who were the first European explorers to see the lake, it was shortly renamed "Lac des Hurons" in honor of the indigenous community who lived on the shore of the lake. Huron boasts the region's longest shoreline at 3,827 miles long, largely due to the lake's large number of islands. Huron has thirty thousand islands, including the world's largest freshwater island, Manitoulin.

Shipwreck Alley

Filled with rocky shoals and frequently visited by treacherous weather, Lake Huron contains an estimated one thousand shipwrecks. The area near Alpena, Michigan, is known as Shipwreck Alley and is the final resting place of an estimated two hundred boats. The Thunder Bay National Marine Sanctuary, operated by the National Oceanic and Atmospheric Administration, covers 4,300 square miles of the lake and contains at least one hundred known shipwrecks. The identified wrecks mirror the history of contemporary travel on the Great Lakes, ranging from wooden steamers launched in the 1840s to a modern five-hundred-foot steel freighter. On the Canadian side of Shipwreck Alley,

Fathom Five National Park protects twenty-two known wrecks. Divers on both sides of the lake continue to search for missing ships in hopes of solving nautical mysteries.

Extreme Weather

Lake Huron was struck with two history-making storms in the twentieth century. The Great Storm of 1913, also known as the White Hurricane, raged through the Great Lakes from November 7–10, 1913. The storm was an extratropical cyclone that combined blinding snow squalls with winds of up to 90 miles per hour and thirty-five-foot waves. It barreled through four of the five Lakes, sparing southmost Lake Ontario. Over the course of the storm, over 250 died and nineteen ships were destroyed. Lake Huron was the most impacted by the storm; nine of the twelve ships that sunk in the storm were on Huron, and 194 sailors were lost beneath the lake's waves. Later in the century, another weather pattern moving north from the Gulf of Mexico created the first-ever recorded tropical cyclone in the Great Lakes. Building over a series of September days in 1996, the cyclone eventually formed a nineteen-mile-wide eye on Lake Huron and brought with it flooding rains but no fatalities.

Mythical Monster

Like many of the other Great Lakes, Huron is linked to water monsters. Mishipeshu, an Ojibwe word meaning "Great Lynx," is said to live in an underwater lair near the mouth of the Serpent River, located on the Canadian side of the lake. This creature, who has a cat-like face and paws, dragon-like scales and spikes, and a long, serpentine tail, is part of the culture of many of the indigenous communities who lived in the Great Lakes region. Thought to be the master of the underwater realm, the creature was believed to seize people in the lake and drag them under the water, causing them to drown. He is also the source of storms on the lake, causing the heavy waves and whirlpools that sink ships. It is also his hand that controls the appearance of disorientating dense fog and breaks the ice on the lake beneath the feet of unlucky travelers.

Often depicted with copper horns or tail, Mishipeshu owns the copper and megis shells, also known as cowrie shells, in Lake Huron but shares them with humans as gifts. Dangerous, but not evil, Mishipeshu tales often show a foil relationship between the underwater panther and the Thunderbirds. While an important part of the history and culture of the region, there are few modern claims of Mishipeshu sightings.

THE STRUGGLE TO SURVIVE: SS *ASIA* (1873–1882)

"In the sweet by and by, we shall meet on that beautiful shore," they sang as they watched that enticing slice of land on the horizon grow ever nearer, their boat drifting in the waves. Waterlogged and weary, they sang on, each note a prayer for deliverance from their peril. They sang to keep their spirits up and to stay awake; the floor of their wooden boat was already lined with the corpses of exhausted men who closed their eyes to rest and drifted into eternal sleep. Numbed by cold, weakened by battling hurricane-force winds, and ravenous after days without food, they sang on.

Captain John Savage managed to fill the SS *Asia*, a wooden paddle wheeler, to overflowing when he shoved off around midnight of September 13, 1882. Onboard was the largest number of passengers the ship had ever carried; each of the ship's thirty staterooms was filled, each cabin and berth was occupied, and cots lined the dining room and sitting rooms. The unlucky claimed a spot of carpeted floor in one of the common rooms, and those who booked steerage passage found spots to sleep during the 200-mile trip from Collingwood to French River among the boxes in the cargo hold. There was likely little room, as the ship was hauling so much cargo that boxes and crates spilled out of the hold and onto the hurricane deck of the 136-foot boat and the

A painting of the sidewheeler, SS Asia   **Detroit Publishing Company, Library of Congress**

steerage passengers were competing for space with a loosely corralled herd of horses.

Savage smiled at the chaos, knowing this would be his most profitable run at the helm of the *Asia.* The flat-bottomed riverboat was dangerously overfilled, carrying an estimated one hundred passengers on a ship designed to carry forty. Significantly deficient in both life jackets and lifeboats for the number of people onboard, the *Asia* was denied a license to sail, but the captain was undeterred. Despite the lack of license and storm warnings, Savage thought the rewards outweighed the risks, as it was a week before the storm season typically began. Believing the odds were with him, he ignored the rapidly lowering barometer, the gulls seeking shelter on land, and the low-flying night-hawks and set sail for what was to be the most lucrative run of the season.

The winds were high when the ship left port, but Savage believed that they would die down once the anticipated rain began. It rained through the night, but instead of calming, the winds increased to a roar. On land, the punishing winds were uprooting mature trees, and on Lake Huron, the whitecapped waves battered the top-heavy *Asia* relentlessly. Seasick passengers braced themselves as best they could as the ship pitched and rolled in the powerful waves. Too far from shore to seek shelter, the *Asia* was forced to fight the now hurricane-force winds and waves.

As the storm raged on, the crew struggled to keep the ship afloat. With her engines running at full force in an attempt to move through the heavy waves, the crew began to throw cargo overboard in an attempt to keep the top-heavy boat above waves that were later described as appearing to be "rolling mountains" of water. The terrified horses, whose stamping, jumping, and frenzied whinnies were increasing the rising panic in the passengers, were released into the water with the discarded cargo. The sun began to rise on the lake, illuminating the calamity and showing no hint of a reprieve from the relentless storm.

While wave after wave crashed over the deck, the crew began to distribute the few life jackets onboard the ship. Eighteen-year-old Christie Ann Morrison tightly fastened the flotation device she was given and went in search of her cousin, First Mate John McDonald. It was nearly eleven in the morning, and the ship began to break apart. The ship was tossing violently in the waves, its wild lurching throwing the girl repeatedly to the ship's floor, but she persevered and eventually found him. His grave face confirmed her fears; the ship was going down. Checking the straps of her flotation device, he urged her to jump into a lifeboat as soon as the crew lowered them. As the cousins spoke, panicked passengers, including seventeen-year-old Duncan Tinkis and his uncle, James, lined the decks of the ship, all vying for their last chance at survival: a spot in one of the three lifeboats the *Asia* carried. The only sound that could be heard over the thunderous sound of the waves pummeling the ship was the frightened wails of the passengers. Some cried while others knelt in prayer. Dazed men, seemingly accepting they would not survive, gathered their families near and waited for the water to claim them.

When the crew untied a lifeboat and lowered it into the water, Christie jumped into the storm-tossed water toward the boat. She pulled herself into the boat, as did Duncan. The younger Tinkis scoured the waves in search of his uncle but could not find him among those clinging to pieces of timber and other wreckage in a desperate bid to remain afloat.

The crew lowered another lifeboat into the water, and it was instantly dashed into pieces by the unrelenting waves. The third boat, dangerously overfilled with panic-stricken passengers, overturned in the waves, ejecting its passengers before disappearing beneath the storm-churned water. The eighteen passengers in the remaining lifeboat watched in terror as those tossed from the lifeboat floundered in the water, grabbing anything within reach, including each other, in an attempt to keep their heads above the powerful waves. Amid that chaos, at eleven-thirty Thursday morning, the SS *Asia*, with her engines still running, sank to the bottom of Lake Huron.

The small lifeboat that remained above the waves was tossed in the angry waves, overturning itself repeatedly. Each time the small group of survivors was upended into the water, another person remained under the waves. Equipped with just a single oar, the increasingly smaller group was adrift and at the mercy of the storm. Morrison, the only woman in the boat, wound the ropes attached to the lifeboat around her slim frame, a strategy that kept her with the boat each time it rolled over in the wave. Others clung to the side of the ship to stay with her when she overturned and were struck by the wooden boat each time they were plunged into the lake. Bloodied and battered, the men could do little other than cling tightly to the boat and bail out the vessel that refilled with each wave that crashed over the exhausted group. As the hours passed, their number continued to dwindle and the sun set, and the small group did what they could to stay awake and alive through a night adrift on the open water.

With darkness came a drop in temperature that left the group numb with cold. As the boat drifted in the night, Christie and Duncan, strangers to each other before entering the same lifeboat, and the remaining survivors—Captain Savage, shipmate McDonald, and a passenger, Mr. Little—huddled together for warmth. Beneath their

Survivor Christie Ann Morrison **WikiCommons**

seats were the bodies of those men who died of exhaustion. The small group sang into the night, the chorus of voices growing smaller until only three remained. The captain, overcome with fatigue, let his eyelids close and ceased his singing. Duncan shook the man to rouse him back into consciousness, but the captain collapsed into the boy's arms, dead. The hopeful survivors, determined to live, fought sleep and the cold until the sun rose.

At daybreak, the pair saw Byng Inlet and the uninhabited islands that are scattered in the eastern part of Georgian Bay at what they estimated to be ten miles away. The boat drifted in the now calm waves until it reached Point aux Barrie around eleven in the morning. After a harrowing eighteen hours in open water, Christie and Duncan, the SS *Asia*'s sole survivors, washed ashore. As happy as the pair were to be on land, their ordeal was far from over. Weak, injured, and hungry, the pair were miles away from aid.

The pair pulled the corpses from the lifeboat and laid them on the beach. Without two oars, their boat was useless to them, and they could see no buildings where they could seek shelter. Overcome with hunger and exhaustion, the teens collapsed on the beach, fearful they escaped the monstrous storm only to die on that isolated beach. With nowhere to go and no rescue ship on the horizon, a discouraged Christie and Duncan spent a cold night clinging to each other on the beach, just yards from the corpses that once shared their lifeboat. They slept fitfully, their empty stomachs growling in protest and haunted in dreams by the horrors they experienced over the last two days.

Before the sun rose on Saturday morning, Duncan determined if they were to survive, they needed to seek help. Christie, hampered by an injury to her leg and overcome with exhaustion, was unable to accompany Duncan on this journey. Tinkis, with a gash to the head, covered in bruises, and on his third day without food, walked into the dark woods in search of aid. Stumbling through the dense forest with nothing to light his way and no path to follow, Duncan soon became disoriented. He trudged along for hours, tripping over tree roots hidden by brush and scratched by thorny bramble, only to find himself again on a beach. Disappointed and confused, he screamed for Christie, trying to find his way back to her. She could hear his cries but was too weak to respond. He eventually found his way back to Morrison and the boat, returning more exhausted and no closer to safety than when he began. The teens endured a second cold and hungry night on that desolate beach, wondering if their prayers to return safely home would be answered.

Dawn broke on another cold, wet, and hungry day for the teens. As the hours crept by that Sunday morning, they spotted something in the distance. Uncertain if delirium had begun, they turned to each other to confirm they were seeing the same thing: a sail in the distance. Elated, Duncan sprung up and grabbed the single oar from the lifeboat. Tearing off his wet, sand-covered jacket, he tied the ragged coat to the oar, swinging it wildly in the air. That speck of sail in the distance was their salvation, and they did everything they could to get the boat to sail their way.

As the boat neared, they saw it was not the rescue boat they imagined but instead a small skiff being paddled by an indigenous man. The duo traded Duncan's gold watch for a ride to Parry Sound. The famished teens ate the only food the man had on his boat, "fat pork" and "chock dog," later declaring it the best meal of their lives.

Once the teens arrived at Parry Sound, they discovered they were the only survivors of the wreck. Due to the loss of the passenger and crew manifests in the wreck, no one knows for certain the number of lives lost on the SS *Asia*; the number is commonly cited as 123 but sometimes appears as high as two hundred souls. The pair were hailed as heroes upon their miraculous return, and their harrowing tale made front-page news across the country. The courageous teens fully recovered from their ordeals within a week.

The celebrity of the shipwreck survivors was tempered by the mourning of the hundreds of families who lost loved ones in the terrible storm. Boats had been sent to recover the bodies of those lost, with many of them washing up on the south shore of Manitoulin Island. Duncan was devastated to learn his uncle's body had not yet been recovered, and he could not bear the thought of the man's corpse bobbing in the waves. As soon as he was able, he gathered two friends and sailed off to the Island to find his uncle, James Tinkis.

The young men hugged the shoreline in search of bodies and discovered four corpses wearing *Asia* lifebelts on the beach. The trio recognized one of the men as fellow islander Mr. Bucknell, who was joined by two deckhands and one unknown lady, but there was no Uncle James, so the search continued. Along another shoreline, they discovered the decaying body of *Asia* passenger Freddie Duncan. This find was significant as there was a reward for the recovery of the fourteen-year-old boy's remains, so the young men boxed up Freddie's body and reunited it with his mother. Despite repeated efforts, Duncan was not able to locate his beloved uncle.

Duncan was not the only one looking for those lost in the wreck. Seekers made a stop at Lonely Island to recover the lost. When the group spoke with the island's lighthouse keeper, Dominic Solomon, he claimed not to have found anything washed up from the *Asia*. As they looked around, they discovered a number of rotting corpses on the small island's shoreline. As they examined the body of a woman whose flesh was so decayed that she was unrecognizable, they noticed impressions on the bloated body's neck and finger where it appeared jewelry had been removed. The group stormed the lighthouse, forcibly conducting a search where they discovered the missing jewelry and a number of other items from the ship, including three *Asia* life preservers that carried the foul odor of rotting flesh. The group left the island with the looted items and the bodies, but none of them were James Tinkis.

The community acted quickly to assign blame for the disaster, conducting a coroner's inquest just days after the boat sank. The calamity was blamed on Captain Savage and focused on his decision to ignore warnings of inclement weather. The tragic loss of life was not entirely in vain; many credit the sinking of the SS *Asia* as the catalyst for the creation of a nautical survey of the Great Lakes to ensure safer passages for all those who sail the Lakes. To this day, the remains of *Asia* have yet to be discovered.

WHITE CLOUD ISLAND'S RESTLESS SOULS: SS *JANE MILLER* (1879–1881)

Where was she? For 136 years, the only traces that remained of the lost SS *Jane Miller* were some air bubbles in a discolored spot of water in Lake Huron and a scattering of wreckage that washed up on White Cloud Island. Given up as sunk in the days after she went missing, it was presumed all aboard met their watery graves that stormy night of November 25, 1881. No bodies from the *Miller* were ever recovered, and if you believe the lore of White Cloud Island, it appears those on board that night who now lie beneath the waves do not rest peacefully.

It was a cold night on the Georgian Bay as the seventy-eight-foot passenger and cargo steamer made her way to Manitoulin Island. The small ship, known as a "coaster," was used to access the small harbors and inlets on the bay. Both she and her captain had a reputation on the lake. The ship was established to be "cranky," meaning she was unstable in the water because she was top-heavy. Her captain, Andrew Port, was noted as a sailor who took chances and underestimated the often-volatile weather on the lake. Port named his twenty-four-year-old son, Richard, as his second-in-command and his purser was his fifteen-year-old son, Frederick. With the only officers aboard calling the ship's captain "dad," it is unknown if they had much influence regarding the risks the captain was willing to take on the water.

The winds roared down from the north, churning the waves as snow filled the skies. She rolled violently in the gale-force winds and had started taking on water. It took more fuel for the small ship to fight through the rough weather, and she was quickly depleting her supply of the cordwood she used for fuel. In need of more wood to make it to her final destination, Port stopped in Big Bay that night. By this time, the snow was coming down in sheets, obscuring visibility. At the dock, Port discovered they did not have enough wood for him to refuel the ship. Instead of stopping for the night, the captain departed fifteen minutes later for the nearby Spenser's Dock in search of more wood.

With just four miles to travel, the ship sailed back into the howling gale. Her deck was packed with cargo that was stacked well over the waterline, and she had little weight in her hold, which caused the top-heavy ship to rock violently in the waves. The passenger area of the ship was sealed up tight against the storm, protecting those on board from the winds and waves that blew over the *Miller*, but those protections made a quick exit from the cabin impossible. On shore, people waiting for the arrival of the steamer *Wiarton Belle* saw the lights of a boat they presumed to be the *Jane Miller* in the distance within an hour of when she left Big Bay. For a moment, a swirl of snow obscured the onlooker's vision, and when the gust passed, the ship was gone. That fleeting glimpse of the steamer was the last known sighting of the storm-tossed ship, which carried an estimated twenty-five to thirty passengers and crew aboard.

Shortly after the *Miller* disappeared, the tug *Tommy Wright* was sent to search for her. The *Wright* dragged the area but found no signs of the boat. Later, the tug came across some large air bubbles rising to the surface of the lake, and the water surrounding the bubbles was a different hue, which are both telltale signs that a ship sank in the area. The men followed the tide from the air bubbles to the shore in search of clues regarding the missing ship. Washed ashore on White Cloud Island, the men discovered a few of the crewmen's caps, some tubs of butter, scraps

On November 25, 1881, the steamer Jane Miller *sank in the Georgian Bay with the loss of twenty-eight passengers and crew.*   **Lake Erie's Yesterdays OhioLINK Digital Resource Commons**

of a ship, and, most telling, two oars marked with the name of the *Jane Miller*.

Not a single body was recovered from the *Miller*, allowing for a sliver of belief that something happened to the ship other than a sinking from the cranky ship rolling over in the storm. In the days following the disappearance of the ship, newspapers kept Georgian Bay communities informed of the search for the *Miller*. As the story unfolded, the local media acknowledged Captain Port's skills and experience, while lambasting his judgment for sailing in the storm on an overloaded ship. The bay towns mourned the loss of those on board, the known, and the ones who remain nameless because the passenger names were not recorded.

In time, stories spread around the islands that those who died on the *Jane Miller* were restless in death. Adding credence to these tales were a group of hunters who were camping on White Cloud Island in 1907. While relaxing in front of their campfire, the men heard the shill cries of a terrified woman. The voice screamed out, "Help me! God save us!" The hunters followed the voice, and it led them to the shore of the island. In the moonlight they could not see any person or vessel, but the cries for help continued. At daybreak, the men retraced their steps to discover whether darkness hid a woman in danger, but again, they could find nothing on land or in the water that indicated that anyone was in the area with them. They shared their experience when they returned to the mainland, and the story was met with knowing nods; the main-landers had heard these stories countless times before. The hunters were told of the missing ship and the belief that the panicked cries are often heard at night. The men made a record of their experience, and in the years that have followed, several others have claimed to have heard the woman's nocturnal pleas for help.

One-hundred-and-thirty-six years after the *Jane Miller* disappeared, she was rediscovered by three divers at the bottom of Colpoy's Bay, not far from White Cloud Island, where debris from the ship was recovered in 1881. The ship is sitting upright at the limestone base of the bay on the bottom of the lake. Peering inside the sunken ship, the divers suspected they saw human remains still aboard, but they could not be certain since the vessel, and all of its contents, are covered in the invasive zebra mussels. The fingernail-sized freshwater mussels create colonies that spread rapidly and grow several inches thick, obscuring anything beneath their blanket of shells. Perhaps it is those bodies, still trapped aboard the ill-fated boat, whose spirits continue to seek a rescue from Lake Huron's waves.

A WARNING UNHEEDED: WAUBUNO (1865–1879)

November winds whipped the Georgian Bay into a frenzy. The Collingwood streets were empty as people sought shelter from the biting cold. Captain Burkett searched the shore, looking for a break in the weather that would allow him to set sail for Parry Sound. His *Waubuno* was a small, wooden, sidewheel paddler. At fourteen years old, the still sturdy 135-foot steamer was used primarily to ferry cargo and passengers between the small Georgian Bay communities. His ship was loaded with everything from livestock to whiskey, and the passenger cabins were booked; now he just needed the gale to abate. He'd been waiting for days, and he, as well as many of the passengers, were eager to set sail.

There was one passenger who did not share this growing impatience to begin the journey. Kate Daupe, the new bride of Dr. Daupe, had a disturbing dream the night before that left her shaken and wary about the journey ahead. She dreamt the *Waubuno* went down in a storm and all aboard died. The dream frightened her, and as she shared its details with her husband the next morning, she urged him to reconsider their journey. Bound for McKellar Village where the doctor would begin a new practice, Kate suggested the newlyweds forgo the boat trip and travel to their new home by train. She made this request knowing all

The sidewheel paddle steamer that conveyed passengers and freight to the small coastal towns in the Georgian Bay **Lake Erie's Yesterdays OhioLINK Digital Resource Commons**

of the couple's possessions, and everything needed to outfit the new medical practice, had already been loaded onto the ship.

Her husband, unwilling to sacrifice the cost of the already purchased tickets and shipping fees, did what he could to soothe her mind. As they discussed her dream, Burkett overheard the conversation and joined the couple. The captain reassured her that he would not set sail unless it was safe to do so and promised her the journey would not end in tragedy. Pacified but not convinced, the woman reluctantly agreed to continue their voyage on the *Waubuno*.

The wind howled through the night, bringing with it snow. Many of the passengers assumed the ship would again be forced to remain in port due to bad weather, so they elected to spend the night on land, rather than riding the rolling waves in one of the ship's cabins. The Daupes, along with several others, made the thrifty choice to spend the night in their cabins, believing the ship would set sail the next morning. Burkett was anxious to begin the journey; it was the end of the sailing season, and he had deliveries that needed to be made before the winter's ice would make travel to remote towns on the Bay impossible. There was still money to be made before the close of the season, and Burkett was determined to seize these opportunities. Restless, he woke the crew at three in the morning and told them to prepare to set sail. One crewman was sent into town to rouse passengers staying at the nearby hotel. Groggy and irritated, the travelers hastily pulled on their clothes and rushed to the dock. The fierce wind stung their faces, and they watched high waves lash at the ship as they waited to board. Determined to leave without delay, the captain did not wait for all ticketed passengers to arrive on the dock, and the *Waubuno* was on her way to Parry Sound within the hour.

Twenty-four people sailed out of Collingwood in the early morning hours of November 22, 1879. In the rush to leave, there was no effort to locate passengers who chose overnight accommodations in any place other than the Globe Hotel. Staying onshore was also the wheelsman scheduled on the run, George Playter, who chose not to follow the passengers onto the dock and instead sent word to the captain that the sailing season had come to an end for him. Burkett was undeterred at the loss of the wheelsman; he was skilled behind the wheel and would take over for the missing crew member. As she sailed through the wind and the snow in the pre-dawn hours, she was spotted about eighteen miles from Collingwood by the Christian Island lightkeeper. The man observed that, despite the heavy waters and increased snow, the *Waubuno* was holding her own and moving through the gale. It was the last time anyone would ever see the wooden steamer again.

When the *Waubuno* did not arrive at Parry Sound that day, it was assumed that the ship found a safe harbor to wait out the storm. When the snow cleared, and there was still no sign of the boat, a tug was sent out to look for the missing steamer. While cruising the South Channel, the tug came across a debris field in the water that included an overturned lifeboat, the ship's ledger, and lifebelts marked with the *Waubuno* name. There was no sign of anyone who had been aboard the ship, living or dead, in the area. There was also no sign of the boat; the only sign the steamer had been in the area were these scattered items bobbing in the waves. Though the searches continued, by November 27, all hope of finding survivors from the assumed wreck had been abandoned.

To this day, no one knows with certainty what happened to the *Waubuno* after she sailed out of the sight of the Christian Island lightkeeper. Some assume she was taken down by a heavy wave, while others suspect the heavy snow forced the captain to sail blindly into an area containing hidden shoals. After the spring thaw of 1880, a hull stripped of its cabins was discovered near Moberly Island that some believe was part of the missing ship, but the piece of wreckage gave no clues to what happened to the boat to which it once belonged. The mystery of the missing ship deepened as word of the strange dream Kate Daupe had before the boat set sail spread around the Bay. The ignored premonition, coupled with the dead who seemingly disappeared without a trace, increased interest in the whereabouts of the small vessel. In the years since she went missing, many have searched for her, hoping to solve the mystery of her fate. While many have claimed to find her, none of the discoveries have been proven to the satisfaction of all. The legend of the ship, the location of her dead, and Mrs. Daupe's terrible dream have all become inextricably woven into the history and lore of Parry Sound.

THE SOLE SURVIVOR: *DANIEL J. MORRELL* (1906–1966)

Dennis Hale was dozing in his bunk. His shift as a watchman aboard the *Daniel J. Morrell* ended at nine-thirty that evening. Shortly after, he undressed to his boxer shorts and climbed between the sheets of his bed with a book. Within an hour he was asleep. It had been a long day for the twenty-six-year-old married father of four. He had missed the boat at the start of its journey and drove hundreds of miles to catch it at its next stop. After a few frantic days, he was finally settling into what would be his last run of the season.

It was a cold November night, and the waves were high on Lake Huron. Throughout the day, the winds had steadily increased, and after midnight on November 29, 1966, wind gusts were measured at nearly 70 miles per hour. Twenty-five-foot waves crashed over the 580-foot-long steel freighter, but the rough weather did not alter the onboard routine. Arthur Crawley, the ship's captain, had been in radio contact with the *Morrell*'s sister ship, the *Edward Y. Townsend*, throughout the day. The massive ships were both struggling against the November Witch but were holding their own against the waves; both ships had been in worse storms in the past and came out unscathed. Just after midnight, Crawley let the *Townsend* know that the *Morrell* was twenty-five miles north of Harbor Beach, Michigan, and was heading for safe harbor in Thunder Bay to wait out the storm. It was the last message ever sent from the *Daniel J. Morrell*.

Sometime around two in the morning, Hale was awakened by a loud thump. For a moment, he thought it was the ship's anchor and was prepared to roll over and go back to sleep when he heard a second hard thump that he would later describe as sounding like a "cannon going off." The ship's lights flickered for a moment, then went out, plunging Hale into darkness. Before he had a chance to consider what was happening, the emergency alarm sounded, filling the darkness with the incessant clanging of the hammer against the bell. Hale leapt from bed, grabbed his life jacket, and ran toward the deck.

As he moved through the boat, another sailor noticed Hale wearing only boxer shorts and his life jacket and urged Hale to put on more clothes; the alarm wasn't a drill, and Hale would need more protection. Hale fumbled through the darkness on his way back to his room, dragging his hands along the hallway wall as he counted the number of doors until he found his cabin. Feeling around the blackened room, he was able to find his woolen peacoat but could not locate his pants or shoes. The alarm continued to sound, reminding him there was no time left to spare, so he gave up his search and put on the coat before he ran out to the deck. As he joined the other sailors, his bare feet moved through the snow and ice that was gathering on the deck of the ship. The 70-mile-per-hour winds stung his bare skin as he heard the news: The ship was breaking in two. The bow and the stern had separated, and the ship was still afloat, but it wouldn't be for long. The men were told to climb onto one of the two rafts aboard the ship, then tie themselves to the raft in case they were swept off the vessel by the twenty-five-foot waves that were tearing apart the *Morrell*. As the ship sank into the thirty-four-degree water, the rafts were intended to float free of the ship.

The men clung to the crowded pontoon rafts, the howling winds carrying sharp shards of snow that stung their exposed skin. They learned that the second thud they had heard was the sound of the electrical lines snapping in half. The ship's radios were powered through the

The steamer Daniel J. Morrell *in the Soo Locks, 1936* **WikiCommons**

electric lines and there had been no time to send out a mayday signal before the lines were severed. No one knew the boat was in trouble, and there was no other ship on its way to rescue the crew. They heard rivet after rivet explode out of the ship's seams as it twisted in the waves. The sound of tearing steel mimicked that of an anguished cry and joined the clang of the alarm bell and roar of the storm. Amid the chaos, the ship broke in half, and the men were unprepared for what happened next. Hale remembers clutching the steel bar of the raft as "the stern, still powered by its engines, was facing us and it started to run into the bow section, ramming up on the side." As the back of the ship struck the front of the ship, the impact from the collision hurled the rafts and its occupants in the stormy waters. In just fifteen minutes from the time the alarm first sounded, the men were plunged into the frigid waves and began their fight for survival.

Hale was tossed into the water, unsure of which direction to swim to reach the surface. Fighting his way through the water, he managed to break through the waves, gasping for breath. Struggling to keep his head above water, he spotted the raft in the distance. Each stroke toward the craft was an effort, but he continued to swim until he grabbed onto the wooden edge of the raft. Exhausted and unsure if he had the strength to pull himself onto the raft, he felt hands grab him and drag him aboard the raft. There were two other sailors aboard the raft, and there was no sight of the other raft or any other crewmen in the water. As the three men scanned the dark waves for signs of life and listened intently for cries for help, they spotted a fourth sailor in the water. They pulled the man onto the raft, and the four men huddled together in an attempt to keep warm as they watched the waves for other survivors.

The storm-soaked men braved the sub-freezing temperatures as snow squalls blew into the area. Through the blinding snow, the men set off flares, in hopes of attracting aid. They tried to use the spent flare gun to warm themselves, but they could not feel its heat on their cold-numbed hands. Ice formed over the men as their raft was tossed in the waves. Just after daybreak, two of the four men would freeze to death on the raft. The light of day brought no new comforts; there were no other ships on the horizon, and the storm continued to rage on. The two remaining men were clinging to life, in pain and drifting in and out of consciousness. So cold they could scarcely move, they waited for a rescue.

On shore, no one knew the *Morrell* sank the night before. The ship had been out of communication since just after midnight, but so had many other ships who were on the lake during the storm, as heavy winds snapped antennas and ice broke wires needed for radio transmissions. That day, the *Morrell*'s sister ship made a refueling stop and discovered a crack that ran through the boat, mirroring what had happened to the *Morrell* the night before. The *Townsend* crew was evacuated unharmed, but no one thought to check on the *Morrell*. Before sunset on November 29, another man on the raft died, leaving just Dennis Hale in his wet peacoat and boxer shorts to survive another night in the storm, surrounded by three frozen corpses.

It took thirty-six hours until anyone realized something happened to the massive steel freighter. At just after one in the afternoon on November 30, the *G. G. Post* spotted something in the water. As the ship got closer to the object bobbing in the waves, they saw it was a body floating in the water wearing a bright orange life jacket. Pulling the corpse aboard the ship, they observed the body had been in the water for some time, as the hair of the sailor was covered in ice. The life jacket was marked with the name of the *Daniel J. Morrell*. The captain immediately radioed in his discovery and then the search began for the ship and her crew.

The Coast Guard began the search for the missing ship immediately, with planes, helicopters, and boats scanning the area where the *Morrell* was last known to be. After forty hours on the open water, the raft Hale boarded when the ship split in two was discovered. Hale, barely conscious, was airlifted to the Harbor Beach Hospital. The search continued for the other men. Shortly, three more bodies wearing life jackets, all face down in the water, were pulled from the waves. In total, eleven bodies were recovered that day, and the second raft from the ship washed ashore, empty. The storm raged on, but the search continued, in hopes of finding other survivors.

On the first day of December, nine more bodies were recovered, and Dennis Hale was acknowledged as the sole survivor of the wreck. In total, twenty-eight men lost their lives on the *Morrell* that stormy night. Some drowned, others froze to death, and there were a few who were never recovered to determine how they died. The tragedy of the *Morrell* changed the safety standards on the Great Lakes, requiring radios to have emergency back-up power sources and introduced more stringent communication protocols. It was determined the ship broke in half because it was made of brittle steel. Its sister ship cracked but did not break in two that night and was later towed to Europe as scrap. The damaged ship did not reach its destination; instead it broke in half and sank very near the spot where the famed *Titanic* sank.

The lone remaining sailor, Hale, made a miraculous recovery after his death-defying experience. He suffered from severe frostbite and was left with nerve damage, but he avoided the need for amputations. Vowing never again to work on a boat, he remained connected to the lake as he often shared this harrowing tale of survival with maritime enthusiasts, and he later wrote a book about his forty-hour ordeal. Dennis Hale died at age seventy-five, telling his story and remembering his fallen crewmembers until the end of his days.

LAKE MICHIGAN

Lake Michigan has a name derived from the Ojibwa word *mishigami*, which is often translated into "great water." This Great Lake has the distinction of being the only lake in the chain that is entirely contained in the United States. The second largest of the Lakes by volume and the third largest in area, the lake is bordered by Illinois, Indiana, Michigan, and Wisconsin. With an average depth of 279 feet, the lake's deepest point measures in at 925 feet. The deep lake rarely freezes over and boasts the largest freshwater sand dune system in the world.

The Michigan Triangle

There have been an estimated fifteen hundred shipwrecks on Lake Michigan, and some believe that number is attributed to more than just heavy weather and rough water. Spanning from Manitowoc, Wisconsin, in the west to Ludington, Michigan, in the east and Benton Harbor, Michigan, in the south, this area known as the Michigan Triangle has been the source of legend and lore for centuries. Like its more famous counterpart, the Bermuda Triangle, the location has a reputation as an unusual place and has been linked to a number of strange disappearances and unexplained tragedies.

While some claim the area inside the triangle to be a vortex with the capability of altering time and still others claim the holy grail of Great Lakes shipwrecks, *Le Griffon*, is hidden in her depths, the first documented disappearance in the triangle happened in 1891. On May 21, the *Thomas Hume* set sail from Chicago and disappeared without a trace.

Not a board, an oar, or any of the seven crew members who were aboard were ever recovered from the wreck. The mystery of what happened to this ship gnawed at sailors for generations, but no clues were found to explain what happened to the 145-foot boat. The legend of the Michigan Triangle grew stronger in 1921 when a 106-foot wooden schooner, the *Rosabelle*, was discovered upside down in the lake, with no clues as to what happened to the eleven people aboard when she left the dock. It appeared that the ship had been in a collision, yet there was no report of an accident and no other ships working the lake at that time were damaged. What happened to the ship, and the fate of the crew, remains unexplained.

It is when Captain George R. Donner of the *O.M. McFarland* went missing that the legend of the Michigan Triangle gained legions of believers. On April 28, 1937, Donner had spent hours navigating the *McFarland* through an obstacle course of dangerous ice floes. Once the ship was safely in unobstructed waters, the captain retired to his chamber, locking the door from the inside. Hours later, when the captain was called back into duty, the crew found his room still locked but empty. A thorough search of the ship was conducted, but the man could not be found. The ship set sail with a new captain at the helm and returned to port without the man or any idea what happened to him. He was never seen again.

These mysterious disappearances are not limited to boats. In 1950, Northwest Airlines Flight 2501 was diverted from Chicago to Milwaukee due to inclement weather. Minutes after the pilot radioed in permission to land due to technical problems, the plane's signal went out, and the plane disappeared from the controller's radar. The plane, and all fifty-eight people aboard, crashed into the lake and were never recovered. The same night Flight 2501 presumably crashed, there were sightings of strange red lights hovering over the lake, which leads some to believe the disappearance of this plane is linked to UFO activity.

Those who believe there is an unexplained phenomenon in Lake Michigan may have gotten evidence to support their beliefs when an unusual discovery was made. In 2007, Dr. Mark Holley, a professor of underwater archeology at Northwestern Michigan College, and Brian Abbot were conducting a study of the floor of the lake when they happened upon a ring of rocks forty feet below the surface of the waves. The stones are arranged in a manner reminiscent of England's Stonehenge, and artifacts were discovered outside the circle, including a carving that resembles the long-extinct mastodon. While the site, with its stone structures and carvings, has yet to be authenticated, there are those who believe the rock formation has mystical powers and is the source of the strange and unexplained events that have long occurred in the storied region.

LAKE MICHIGAN'S BLEAK WEEK: SS *MILWAUKEE*, SS *WISCONSIN*, AND SS *SENATOR*

In late October 1929, Lake Michigan saw her bleakest week in modern memory. On land, the country was teetering on the edge of financial ruin, with the volatile stock market making dramatic yo-yo dips and climbs before finally crashing on October 29, plunging the nation into the Great Depression. The eyes of the world watched the markets and read the news of the growing unrest around the globe, and the eyes of Wisconsin watched Lake Michigan. The November Witch was already in her full fury, with relentless gales and high waves that splintered piers and washed away beach homes all along the Wisconsin coastline.

Some believe tragedy comes in threes, and that terrible week on the lake did nothing to disprove this superstition. The first tragedy in that bleak week came on October 22. It was the day the SS *Milwaukee*, a stout freighter captained by Robert "Heavy Weather" McKay, went out onto the lake for the last time.

The SS *Milwaukee* (1908–1929)

Captain Robert "Heavy Weather" McKay worked the Great Lakes for more than fifty years. The sixty-seven-year-old Scotch immigrant was a tenacious man known for safely battling through the roughest of seas. He earned his moniker through heroic feats, like the time he spent battling a storm, nose first in the wind, for thirty-eight hours until he could safely seek shelter ashore. McKay followed company orders, and he worked hard to keep his runs on schedule, despite the weather.

The captain maneuvered the SS *Milwaukee* into port on the afternoon of October 22, 1929. He battled gale-force eight winds on the trip from Grand Haven, Michigan, into the Port of Milwaukee. Despite the high waves and strong winds, McKay ordered the freighter to be reloaded for its scheduled trip across the lake. The men loaded the ferry with twenty-seven railcars filled with everything from bathtubs to cheese, as they watched the storm worsen. With the winds now at gale-force nine, many of the sailors assumed the run would be rescheduled until the storm passed. Three sailors were so certain the *Milwaukee* would not sail that they did not even show up to the dock that day; however, McKay was determined to maintain shipping schedules and continued to ready the boat to sail. That he had just crossed the lake successfully hours earlier may have colored his decision to return to Grand Haven. McKay had some reasons to be confident; the steel ship, built in 1903, was a massive 338 feet long and among the sturdiest vessels on the lake.

When the captain sounded the alert that the ship was about to sail, it surprised sailors and onlookers alike. No other ferries in the port were preparing to sail, deciding the weather was too heavy to safely cross the lake. It is not known whether anyone challenged the grizzled leader's command, or if he knew that the storm had intensified to such an extent since he had arrived in Milwaukee that there were reports coming in of intermittent rain squalls and coastline piers being splintered and washed away by the heavy winds. No one knows how many men were aboard the *Milwaukee* when she shoved off that stormy afternoon,

"WI Milwaukee WI Muskegon MI RPPC WONDERFUL Grand Trunk Ferry Lines SS MILWAUKEE Ferry Crashing the Lake MI Surf US Mail Boat AZO66" *UpNorth Memories – Donald (Don) Harrison is licensed under CC BY-NC-ND 2.0*

with reports stating anywhere between forty-seven to fifty-nine sailors, and many sources settling on fifty-two as the number of crew that set sail on the ferry's final run.

US Lightship 95 reported that she spotted the SS *Milwaukee* about three miles east of the Port of Milwaukee at 3:45 p.m. on that fateful afternoon. The massive ferry was seen pitching and rolling heavily in waves that crashed over its hull. The lightship watched the ferry being tossed about for ten minutes until the fog, rain, and high waves obscured her. She was never seen again.

The storm raged on with a fury. The heavy waves destroyed 1,300-ton sections of the concrete breakwater wall near Milwaukee. There were reports along the coast of beachfront homes being washed away by the ravenous waves, and rivers were flooding lakeside towns. The Coast Guard received reports of ships going down in the storm. There was no radio on the SS *Milwaukee*, so it was not known how she was faring in the storm, but the sturdy steel freighter navigated by "Heavy Weather" McKay was the least of anyone's worries that stormy night.

It wasn't until thirty-six hours after the SS *Milwaukee* was due to arrive in Grand Haven that people began to grow concerned about the ferry's whereabouts. Travel delays during storms were quite common, as it is often safer for a vessel to weather the storm, while keeping the winds off her sides, than attempt to navigate the dangerous waters. At this point, the storm had passed, and the *Milwaukee* should have made it to a port by this time. The concerned owners of the ferry had a rescue plane fly over the ship's route on October 24 to see if they could catch sight of the ship, but the pilot could not detect any trace of the massive boat. Soon, clues to the fate of the ferry would appear scattered around the lake.

As boats resumed their routes on the now easy seas, they discovered traces of the *Milwaukee* and her crew. Pieces of what many believed to be the missing ship were spotted north of Racine, and shortly after that dead sailors began to be pulled from the lake. Four men were discovered in the waves, two of them wearing life jackets marked with the name SS *Milwaukee*. By October 26, a lifeboat from the *Milwaukee* was found near Holland, Michigan. Aboard the bobbing boat were four sailors, all of whom reportedly died of exposure and exhaustion. When the Coast Guard joined the search for the *Milwaukee* and her crew, they uncovered a significant clue that washed up on a Grand Haven beach on October 27.

Near an empty *Milwaukee* lifeboat was the message box from the ship. With a design far stronger than the fragile glass bottles used on boats in the past, this metal, water-tight tube was part of the ship's standard equipment and was to be used to communicate information from a ship in distress. The container was opened, and the tightly rolled message was carefully removed. The letter inside read:

> *S. S. Milwaukee*, October 22, '29
> The ship is making water fast. We have turned around and headed for Milwaukee. Pumps are working but sea gate is bent and can't keep water out. Flicker is flooded. Seas are tremendous. Things look bad. Crew roll is about the same as last payday.
> A.R. Sadon, Purser

The message, written at 8:30 p.m., and in the verified handwriting of the purser, filled the men with dread. The ship was fitted with a five-foot sea gate that was meant to prevent water from entering the ship's stern. The gate was damaged and allowing the heavy seas to enter the boat. The flicker, a term that was used for the sailor's below-deck living quarters, was filled with water, and the pumps, designed to keep the inside of the boat dry, could not keep up with all of the water rushing into the ferry. It seemed clear; the SS *Milwaukee* was at the bottom of Lake Michigan.

The entire crew of the *Milwaukee* was lost on October 22, 1929. Of the estimated fifty-two men on the ship for that final voyage, fifteen of the bodies were recovered. One of the men pulled from the waves was wearing a watch that stopped at 9:35 p.m., and it is assumed that it is around that time the *Milwaukee* slipped below the surface. Where she was, and why this tragedy, considered one of the worst ferry wrecks that ever occurred on the Great Lakes, was a matter of a great deal of debate and speculation.

An extensive investigation was launched to determine how this mighty ship went down. The investigation sparked rumors that McKay was a drunk whose impaired judgment doomed the boat and crew— claims that were hotly denied by his wife and close friends. Others speculated that it was the fault of the Grand Trunk Car Ferry Company, with claims that McKay had been forced to make the dangerous run despite the storm. The company refuted these claims by providing evidence that they shared weather reports with their captains, as well as records which indicated that many of their ships remained in port during the storm. The boat passed all physical inspections in the summer of 1929 and was believed to be a sound ship. With the absence of any evidence to the contrary, the investigation concluded that the ship was simply overcome by the storm.

It wasn't until 1972 when the wreck was found just three miles offshore in Fox Point, a northern suburb of Milwaukee, that it could be determined what caused the mighty ferry to lose its battle against the blustery gale. Modern investigators have concluded the damaged sea gate, coupled with the lack of airtight hatches in the boat's belly, were the contributing factors in her sinking. The sinking of the SS *Milwaukee* remains one of the deadliest ferry wrecks ever to occur on the Great Lakes.

The SS *Wisconsin* (1899–1929)

Just a few days later, the freighter SS *Wisconsin* set sail on October 29, 1929. The ship had a complicated history that led many a superstitious sailor to be wary of her. In sailing culture, the belief that it is bad luck to change the name of a ship goes back centuries. The SS *Wisconsin* had many name changes in her life, including a renaming to honor her owner, a man who had drowned during the sinking of the infamous *Titanic*! Beyond the superstitions surrounding the ship's name, this iron-hulled steamer built in 1881 was no stranger to tragedy and death before she finally came to rest at the bottom of the cold, deep lake.

The *Wisconsin*'s early days were not exceptional. In 1882, the ship struck a pier, and the collision tore a twenty-foot hole in the port side of the ship. She was repaired but was docked again in 1885 when she was trapped by ice on the lake, which crushed the ship so tightly that a hole appeared in her hull. She changed hands and was renamed *Naomi* in 1886. She had a few uneventful years on the lake but was then trapped on the lake by ice three times in 1893.

The ship saw its first fatalities as a nightmarish calamity unfolded in the early morning hours of May 21, 1907. The steamer was making a night run from Grand Haven, Michigan, into Milwaukee with sixty passengers when a fire started between the forward decks. A passing ship, the SS *Kansas*, noticed the flames and alerted the *Naomi* she was on fire. The crew began to evacuate passengers at 1:30 in the morning, and the nearby *Kansas*, *Kerr*, and *Saxonia* aided in the rescue. With the lifeboats filled and the flames climbing ever higher, the *Kerr* maneuvered itself as close to the *Naomi* as she dared, to allow those trapped on the deck of the ship to jump from the burning *Naomi* and onto the *Kerr*. While passengers and crew were being evacuated, there were four coal passers trapped in the forecastle.

Onlookers in the nearby boats watched in horror through the portholes of ship's forward at the workmen trapped by flames. The desperate men tried in vain to push their bodies through the narrow portholes, but the effort was fruitless; the holes were too small to allow for an escape. Unable to do anything for the men, the rescued passengers witnessed each of the coal passers fall back into the smoke-filled room, their tortured cries filling the air, as all four men burned to death. Later, it was discovered a fifth man, a passenger who was found badly burned in his berth, also died.

The *Naomi* burned to the waterline that night but was rebuilt and sailed again. She was renamed in 1912 for her owner, Edward Gifford Crosby, who died in the sinking of the *Titanic* in April of 1912. In 1918, the ship saw more death when she served in World War I as a convalescent ship under the name SS *Robert M. O'Reilly*. At the close of WWI, she changed hands again and was briefly known as the SS *Pilgrim*, before finally returning to her original name, SS *Wisconsin*, in 1924.

The year 1929 was shaping up to be another difficult one for the ship. She was struck by lightning on June 19, and she ran into the same heavy storm that took the *Milwaukee* on October 22, causing her to return to the Port of Milwaukee significantly listing to her port side. Once her cargo was unloaded, she righted herself, and it was thought that her list was the result of the storm shifting the cargo and throwing the boat off balance. In retrospect, this assessment was likely incorrect.

The steamer left Chicago and bound for Milwaukee on the evening of October 29, 1929, filled with iron castings, automobiles, and a variety of boxed freight, along with four passengers. The night was a windy one, and as soon as she made it past the breakers, the ship was rolling in the waves. The northwesterly gale was relentless, and the crew was unable to stabilize the boat in the powerful waves. The heavy cargo began to shift, causing the boat to begin to take on water. The *Wisconsin*'s pumps were running at full capacity, but the flooding grew worse. With water still pouring into the firehold, Captain Morrison sent a message at 1:30 in the morning that the ship was flooding and in danger. The ship could be saved, but it needed to be towed into port quickly.

By 2:35 in the morning, Morrison and the crew were stranded in the storm. The *Wisconsin* had taken on so much water that the engines were out, as was all of their auxiliary power. The wind howled in the black night as the ship tossed in the storm while the men waited for the tow to shore. The *Butterfield* had left the Racine port to aid the *Wisconsin*, but the storm caused her to take on too much water, so the *Butterfield* was forced to return without reaching the distressed vessel.

As the ship continued to take on water, it was necessary to evacuate the sinking ship. The significant list of the ship meant only the port side lifeboats could be used, leaving some of the crew without the means to escape.

The four passengers and some of the crew filled the available lifeboats, with others throwing life rafts off the boat and jumping in after the rafts. The Coast Guard had arrived, and some men leapt into the high waves, swimming through the storm to find safety aboard these boats. Soon, all of the lifeboats were overfilled, and there were men still in the water, struggling to survive in the heavy waves. As the crew fought for their lives in the water, a few of the crew elected to stay with the ship and its loyal captain.

After the first of the lifeboats made it to shore, tugs were sent to rescue more men. The desperate crew clung together on sinking rafts, fighting against hypothermia and struggling to keep their heads above the ceaseless waves, waiting for the second wave of lifeboats to arrive.

As the rescue efforts continued, the *Wisconsin* took on more water until she slipped beneath the surface shortly after 6:30 in the morning. As she sunk, the air pressure building in her hull caused an explosion that blew her aft cabin and pilothouse off the ship. Captain Morrison, last seen on the deck of the sinking vessel, was later spotted about twenty-five to thirty feet away from one of the *Wisconsin*'s lifeboats, alive and clinging to a life preserver. The exhausted crew, waiting to be rescued, attempted to row to their leader, but the heavy seas prevented them from reaching the man. They watched from the boat as he was hit in the head by a piece of the boat's wreckage and struck unconscious.

When help arrived, rescuers pulled him onto a lifeboat, but he died on the Kenosha beach.

In the end, fifty-nine men had been rescued, nineteen of whom were seriously injured. Nine men lost their lives in the sinking of the SS *Wisconsin*. It is believed that most of the dead succumbed to exposure. Four victims remained unidentified and unclaimed and were laid to rest on November 2, 1929, in unmarked graves in Kenosha's Green Ridge Cemetery.

The SS *Senator* (1896–1929)

The final tragedy of that bleak week occurred on one of the most superstition-laden nights of the year: All Hallows' Eve. The SS *Senator* was a steel-hulled freighter built in 1896. She was built for hard work, hauling iron ore, coal, and other heavy loads around the Lakes. On October 31, 1929, the ship was loaded with 268 Nash automobiles built in Kenosha on their way to Detroit and then to car dealerships across the Midwest. At the helm was a seasoned sailor, Captain Kinch. It had been a bad week on the Lakes, with the sinking of both the SS *Milwaukee* and the SS *Wisconsin* happening just days before the run. Worried about her father, the captain's daughter pleaded with him to skip this run and stay at home. In an effort to comfort the girl, Kinch reassured her that he was in no danger, stating that the *Senator* was the best steamer on the lake, and they would come to no harm.

The night air was damp, and the fog hung heavily on Lake Michigan, giving the sailors a visibility of only one hundred feet. Mindful of the delivery commitments required of the *Senator*, at 10:30 that night, Kinch sounded the whistle to alert the twenty-seven-man crew that the ship would soon set sail. Conditions were perilous, and the sailors did what they could to cross the fog-enshrouded lake. The crew needed to navigate by sound, as the men could see nothing around them but tendrils of fog. The windows of the freighter were lowered, and the sailors maintained silence, allowing the captain's keen ears to hear every clue that could be gathered about where the boat was and, most importantly, how near they were to any other boats who also dared to venture out on that murky night.

Reports of the journey vary, with some reporting that the north-bound *Senator* sailed at full speed that night, slowing only for the cautionary sounds of foghorn blasts from nearby ships, while others stated the ship moved slowly through the dense fog. What is not debated is that, suddenly and unexpectedly, the freighter met the south-bound SS *Marquette* less than twenty miles off Port Washington that Halloween night. There was a moment of stunned disbelief on both boats as the vessels neared each other, only to be broken by the frantic sound of clanging alarm bells and shouts of "full astern" from both captains. The experienced seamen made the command without a second thought; the order followed maritime protocol, yet this time, following the time-honored rules would prove deadly. The ships quickly turned in intercepting directions, causing the *Senator* to be rammed amidship by the *Marquette*.

The *Senator*'s side had been torn open by the ore-laden *Marquette*. The gash in the side of the ship was well below the waterline, and the boat began to list moments after it was struck. From there, chaos reigned as desperate cries for aid filled the night. The *Senator* was sinking rapidly, and there was no time for the lifeboats to be deployed. With her hull torn, she filled with water, and within minutes, she lay on her port side. Sailors leapt into the icy water, clinging to life preservers or attempting to land on the few rafts that had been released into the water. The collision caused the *Marquette* to release her anchors, offering the men struggling to keep their heads above the choppy waves a chance to save themselves. A few of the *Senator* sailors pulled themselves from the water and began climbing the *Marquette*'s anchor chain, then dropping themselves through the gash in the ship. As the men did what they could to survive, the *Senator* continued to take on water, sinking less than ten minutes after she was struck.

By now, the *Marquette* was also taking on water, and she radioed the Coast Guard that she would attempt a beaching at Port Washington. The water was still filled with men in need of assistance, and fortunately, a nearby fishing tug, the *Delos H. Smith*, heard the tremendous crash and sailed toward the wreck to offer aid. The men had become desperate in the frigid water, their limbs turning blue as they strained to stay above the waves. When the tug cast out lines for rescue, the men frantically scrambled toward them, pushing each other away from the lines in a frenzied bid to save themselves. The tug pulled fifteen live sailors from the water that night.

The panic and terror of the night gave way to painful realities as those on shore began to learn of what happened. The SS *Senator*, and all of her cargo, was on the bottom of the lake. Nine of the twenty-eight crew members on the SS *Senator* died that night, including Captain Kinch and Minnie Gormley, the ship's cook, who managed to jump off the ship but became too exhausted in the icy water to maintain a hold of the raft. Releasing her grip on the raft, the woman quietly slipped below the waves, never to be seen again. It was reported that the captain's daughter, overcome when she discovered her father's fate by reading of it in the newspaper, collapsed upon learning of the news. The SS *Marquette* did make it to shore and lived to sail for years after, but the shadow of that night followed its captain, who many criticized for not doing more to aid the men of the wrecked *Senator*, as an investigation indicated no life rings were thrown, ladders lowered, or lifeboats launched to help the men in the water.

The *Senator* sunk so deeply beneath the waves that she was not rediscovered until 2005. The wreck is considered to be one of the best-preserved wrecks on the Great Lakes because it settled 450 feet below the surface of Lake Michigan. The depth, which is more than three hundred feet deeper than the recreational limits for scuba divers, made it impossible to locate without the aid of modern equipment. The frigid water and the absence of natural light helped protect the ship and its contents from breaking down in the water. This wreck, which was listed on the National Register of Historic Places in 2016, is now best known as the location of the largest collection of original Nash automobiles in the world. While the ship's freight was remarkably well preserved, none of her dead were ever recovered. True to the legend, the November

Witch did not give up her dead. They remain, somewhere beneath the tides, never to return.

ROGERS CITY WEPT: SS *CARL D. BRADLEY* (1927–1958)

In 1958, Rogers City, Michigan, had a population of 3,873 people. Home of one of the world's largest limestone quarries, nearly everyone in town earned their living through the business of mining the plentiful stone. The port city was home to a small fleet of freighters that shipped limestone throughout the Great Lakes. The jewel of the fleet was the *Carl D. Bradley*, a self-unloading limestone carrier. For years she was the undisputed queen of the Lakes; at 639 feet, the record-breaker was the largest, fastest ship sailing the inland sea. She was also at the heart of the worst tragedy that ever befell Rogers City.

It was supposed to be the last run of the season. The empty ship was returning from a delivery in Gary, Indiana, and was bound for Manitowoc, Wisconsin, to spend the winter in dry dock to undergo some much-needed repairs, including the replacement of the ship's thirty-one-year-old cargo hold. The vessel had many years of service ahead of her, but her holds leaked, and the ship's rivets popped off by the bucketful when she twisted in the waves during heavy weather. The crew frequently joked that "rust is about all that's holding the *Bradley* together." That year she had a rough season; she ran aground twice and had been docked for three months. Despite her shape and her patchwork of repairs, she had passed both her spring and fall Coast Guard safety inspections, yet the time had come to overhaul the vessel.

The crew was looking forward to the end of the season on November 17, 1958, when they left their load in Gary. Most of the men onboard lived in Rogers City, and they were eager to return home to their families and celebrate Thanksgiving. When they awoke on the morning of November 18 and looked across the horizon, they discovered they were not bound for the Wisconsin port, as had been planned. Captain Roland Bryan received a call from the boat's owner that there was one more load of stone to be delivered before the season closed and that he should change his course and return to the quarry. The November weather that day was already heavy, but the seasoned veteran who had been sailing since age fourteen was not concerned. The *Bradley* hadn't had a good season, and this additional run would help increase the vessel's profitability. Bryan was a company man; he did what he was told to do, and he trusted the *Bradley* to get them there in any weather.

The crew trusted the *Bradley* as well. Throughout the day the ship was battling strong winds and high waves, but the sailors were unconcerned. By late afternoon the winds were howling at 65 miles per hour and thirty- to forty-foot waves were cresting over the deck of the ship. The outer decks were pelted with sleet and snow, but with the exception of a few grumbles regarding the extended sailing season, there was no deviation from the routine operation of the ship. At 5:20 that evening, First Mate Elmer Fleming radioed the ship's estimated arrival time to the Rogers City port. Within ten minutes of this routine transmission, the massive steel freighter would break apart and toss the crew into the arms of the November Witch.

The tragedy began with a tremendous boom. Deckhand Frank Mays was startled by the sound that was followed by a shudder that ran through the boat with a bone-shaking vibration. Within moments, the crew noticed the ship's half aft sagging. The ship's radio crackled to life as the first mate shouted into the microphone, "Mayday! Mayday! Mayday! This is the *Carl D. Bradley*, our position is approximately twelve miles southwest of Gull Island. We are in serious trouble! We're breaking up!" There was a tear forming in the top deck, and sparks flew as the waves slammed the two sides of the severing ship against each other.

Captain Bryan ordered the engines to halt while he sounded the alarm for the crew to abandon the ship. The *Bradley* was breaking in two.

Water rushed into the widening crack in the ship as the men scrambled to locate life jackets. Quickly, the separation grew so wide that the men in the forward of the boat were stranded without access to the lifeboats stored in the stern. As the ship split, the bow filled with water, and the ship began to sink. The wail of the ship's alarm was joined by the grating of metal, the shrieking of the 70-mile-per-hour winds, and the roar of the two-story-high waves that punished the breaking vessel. Weakened and low in the water, the ship was hit by a massive wave so powerful that it swept all thirty-five crewmen off the ship.

Plunged into frigid water, the men were separated by the violent waves. Mays reached the life raft that was tossed into the water moments before he was pulled into the storm. He climbed on the small wooden structure without oars and called into the darkness, searching for his crewmates. He could hear cries for help, but in the darkness he could not see anyone and was not even able to determine how far away from the raft the struggling sailors were. Elmer Fleming swam through the waves and appeared at the edge of the raft. Mays spotted him and pulled him onboard. They screamed into the wind, seeking out others, and were soon joined by Gary Stzelecki and Dennis Meredith. The men, soaked by the forty-six-degree water and ravaged by the blasts of arctic wind, huddled together as they stared into the darkness looking for the others.

In the distance, a German cargo ship, the *Christian Satori*, was also battling the storm. The ship had not heard the *Bradley's* call for help, but it was aware the *Bradley* was sailing within a few miles of her. The startled crew heard an explosion over the roar of the wind that was accompanied by a column of flame that burned red, yellow, and white. In moments, heavy smoke obscured the tower of flame. Then, the *Bradley* suddenly disappeared from the *Satori's* radar. When the smoke cleared, all traces of the ship were gone. The *Satori* went to investigate the explosion. The ship was just four miles away from the *Bradley's* last known location, but the storm hindered the boat's movements so

"SS CARL D BRADLEY & Tugs RPPC SHIPWRECK DISASTER Lake Michigan
1958 33 of 35-man crew were dead vessel delivering limestone for Mi Limestone & Chem
11" UpNorth Memories - Don Harrison is licensed under CC BY-NC-ND 2.0*

severely that it took the cargo ship an hour to reach their goal. When
they arrived, the crew scanned the dark, stormy expanse of water, with
their only light source, flares, searching for stranded sailors.

The men on the raft saw the explosion as well. It happened when
the cold water finally reached the ship's hot boilers. The blast filled the
air with acrid smoke that burned the men's eyes and stung their lungs.
When the smoke dissipated, they spotted the ship lights of the *Satori*
on the horizon. As the ship neared, they tried to light the final flare on
the raft. Despite repeated attempts, the waterlogged flare refused to
ignite. The men prayed the ship would spot their small raft through the
black night.

The *Satori* crew stood on the deck in the freezing rain and searched
the pounding waves for any sign of life. They could hear nothing above
the roar of the storm. In time, they called off the search and reported
what they witnessed to the Coast Guard. Before eight in the evening,
the captain reported, "I believe all hands are lost. No lifeboats visible."
The ship returned to its set course, and the men on the raft watched the
Satori sail away, knowing they had not been seen. The men focused their

efforts on surviving the night with the hope that they would be found when daylight returned.

Deckhand Dennis Meredith was sleeping when the captain sounded the alarm to abandon the boat. He fled the ship in just light clothing and still had bare feet when he strapped on his life vest and was swept into the lake. When he was pulled aboard the raft, he appeared to be in shock. The other men, more warmly dressed, edged closer to him in an attempt to protect him from the elements. The sailors slipped their fingers between the wooden slats of the life raft in a desperate bid to stay on the small craft being tossed in the waves. Caught by cresting waves, the raft repeatedly flipped, plunging the men back into the cold water. It was a greater struggle to pull themselves back onto the raft each time they were thrown off. After the third upset, Mays and Fleming climbed aboard, joining Stzelecki, who was already on the raft, when they spotted Meredith in the water. The men grabbed Meredith from the lake, and they could see the man was dead. Together, they released his body back into the waves. Dennis Meredith was never recovered from the lake.

While the men struggled to survive, the Charlevoix Coast Guard Station had heard the Mayday call and scrambled to get aid to the fallen ship and her crew. Most of the stations in the area were either too far from the men or had ships that could not handle the heavy winds and waves of the brutal November storm. Finally, at one-thirty in the morning, a US Coast Guard cutter from Sturgeon Bay, Wisconsin, arrived at the *Bradley*'s last known location after battling the relentless storm for hours. When the cutter arrived, the small raft was nowhere to be found. The search continued throughout the remainder of the night, and by daybreak, the cutter would be joined in the search by a number of commercial ships and search aircraft.

Word quickly spread through Rogers City that the *Carl D. Bradley* was in trouble. Twenty-six of the thirty-five men aboard the *Bradley* lived in Rogers City. Townspeople came in droves to the Coast Guard station and stayed the night, waiting for word on the fate of the crew.

Candles were lit and prayers sent for the safe return of the fathers, husbands, sons, and brothers who worked aboard the fallen vessel.

While the search continued, the wave-tossed raft, propelled by heavy winds, had traveled miles since the *Bradley* sunk. Ice formed on the men as they clung to life. During the long night, the men kept their fingers clenched around the wooden slats of the raft as they curled into themselves to protect their inner organs from the cold. They could feel their bodies growing weaker as the cold enveloped them. At dawn, Stzelecki inexplicably jumped from the raft. Mays and Fleming were powerless to stop him from leaving the raft and watched in shared horror as he jumped into the angry waves. Miraculously, Stzelecki was later pulled from the water alive but died within minutes of his rescue.

The two remaining men lay on the raft, numbed with cold. As they drifted in the waves, they heard the sound of aircraft above them, and they again prayed they would be spotted. This time, their prayers were answered. After fifteen hours on the open water, at 8:37 in the morning, Fleming and Mays were pulled from the lake by the Coast Guard cutter *Sundew*. Still alive, the men learned they had drifted nearly twenty miles from the *Bradley* wreck. The pair were rushed to the hospital where they were reunited with their families.

The thirty-three remaining families held out hope that their sailor was also awaiting rescue somewhere on the lake. As the rescuers searched by land and water for additional survivors, they recovered seventeen dead crew members. Also located was an overturned lifeboat from the ship that showed no evidence of having been occupied. In the days that followed, more debris from the ship was recovered, but no additional survivors were found. Fifteen of the crew were lost beneath the waves and never recovered.

The survival of the shipwrecked men was quickly overshadowed by the death of so many Rogers City residents. The sinking of the *Bradley* left twenty-three widows and fifty-three orphans in the small community. The devastated town mourned for the dead and for those left behind. A mass wake for the lost men was held in the Rogers City High School gym. The funerals for the drowned crew were held at noon on November 22. There was not an open business in the town as its community grieved together at the services.

Soon, sorrow turned to anger, and the families of the dead wanted answers about what happened to the *Bradley*. Since their rescue, Fleming and Mays maintained that the ship sank because it broke in half. The ship's owner, US Steel Corporation (USS), disagreed, countering the ship must have foundered in the storm, declaring the wreck "an act of god." This point was argued in the courts for months and debated on barstools for years. If the ship did break in half, as the survivors claim, USS would be responsible for the wreck due to their failure to maintain the vessel. At stake were millions of dollars, and USS was prepared to do anything needed to avoid responsibility for the wreck.

Coast Guard hearings occurred soon after Fleming and Mays were able to leave the hospital. Questions about Captain Bryan's judgment in sailing in the storm were debated. The safety and maintenance records of the ship were looked at in detail. Despite pointed questions aimed to the contrary, the men were unwavering in their declarations that the ship broke in half in the storm. Vice Admiral A. C. Richmond, the US Coast Guard commandant who led the inquiry, remarked that:

> the extensive renewal of [the] cargo hold…planned by the company for the 1958-8-59 winter lay-up is in itself indicative of wear and deterioration…the fact that the vessel broke up and foundered under conditions which, while severe, she should easily have been able to weather, leads inevitably to the conclusion that the vessel had developed and undetected structural weakness or defect.

USS did not agree with this conclusion and continued the fight to prove the ship was sound when she failed in the storm.

Whether or not the ship split in half, the investigation further determined that a contributing factor to the death toll of the tragedy was the lifesaving equipment on the ship. The cork life jackets given to the crew were fastened only with front laces, and the men struggled to stay in the vests while being tossed in the waves. Forced to use their arms to hold the vest close to their bodies so they would not slip out of the devices, the men used only their legs to propel them through the water and keep their heads above the waves. Experts would later state this exacerbated the crew's exhaustion and likely contributed to crew fatalities. A number of empty, laced-up vests were recovered from the lake, and it was assumed these were worn by men who slipped out of the vests. In the future, life vests would include straps that ran between the legs, as well as around the wearer, to ensure the device would remain fastened to the body. Additionally, the failed flare that was too wet to use when the *Satori* was near enough to rescue the four men was linked as a key factor in the deaths of Meredith and Stzelecki. Soon, lifesaving kits would be required to include parachute flares, which can be used when wet.

The angry families of the dead men accused the company of greed, stating the ship would have bypassed the storm had it gone to Manitowoc for repair, as was originally planned. Accusations flew that the company knew the ship was unsound and put the profits of a single cargo delivery above the lives of the crew. In order to exonerate themselves from responsibility, USS hired the boat the *Penmanta* to locate the ship and investigate the wreck. On April 20, 1959, the wreck was located using an underwater scanner, and the *Penmanta* determined the ship was in one piece. USS published the findings, but the families, who were now also litigants in a case pending against the company, were unconvinced. USS then hired the Global Marine Exploration Company to photograph the sunken ship. USS refused to include impartial witnesses to the exploration of the wreck and would later refuse to share the photos taken on the expedition. The company located the *Bradley* under 375 feet of water and photographed the ship. The exploration company declared the lower hull of the ship was intact, but no other evidence of this conclusion was presented. On December 4, 1959, the company settled the case of the *Carl D. Bradley* for $1.25 million.

The settlement did nothing to end the debate as to what really happened to the *Carl D. Bradley*. She rested in water so deep that it could only be explored by the most advanced dive teams. Buried in deep silt, the ship was obscured by the murky water in which she was submerged. In 1997, an expedition using a remote-operated underwater vehicle was able to reach the ship and record the wreck. Mays, who never wavered in his claims that the ship had broken in half, felt vindicated by the footage, which he believes clearly shows the ship in two pieces. Others who have viewed the footage state the film is inconclusive, as the hull of the ship is buried deep into the floor of the lake, and it cannot be determined whether it is in one or two pieces. It is likely this question will never be answered to the satisfaction of all.

The town of Rogers City still remembers the tragedy that occurred on November 18, 1958, and still mourns for those taken by the lake. To honor the fiftieth anniversary of the sinking, divers recovered the original bell from the *Carl D. Bradley* and replaced it with a replica of the bell that was engraved with the names of the thirty-three men who died aboard the ship. The recovered bell, now restored, is tolled on the anniversary of the sinking in memory of the men who were on their way to pick up one last load of the season.

DEVASTATION ON THE CHICAGO RIVER: THE SS *EASTLAND* (1903–1915)

At the turn of the twentieth century, it took two men four hours to dig a grave: one starting at the head of the plot, and the other at the foot until they met in the middle of the coffin-ready hole. In the days following July 24, 1915, Chicago gravediggers would repeat this four-hour task 844 times. One hole was needed to accommodate each of the dead from the sinking of the SS *Eastland*. Today, the sinking of this ship is considered the worst maritime disaster to ever occur on the Great Lakes, yet the boat never left the dock. The accident took more lives than the Great Chicago Fire and left the westside of Chicago covered in mourning crepe.

The *Eastland* was built to be a fast, luxurious excursion ship; at different times in her career, she was known as both "the Speed Queen" and "the Aristocrat" of the Great Lakes. Despite these flattering monikers, the notoriously unstable boat was also known by another name among those in the maritime community: "the Crank" of the Great Lakes. The 265-foot boat was top-heavy from the time she was built, and the problem only grew worse as she was modified to accommodate more guests and offer more amenities. After the sinking of the *Titanic* in 1912, laws were passed to ensure passenger boats carried enough lifeboats to

"Chicago River – The Eastland *Disaster"* **Wallyg is licensed under CC BY-NC-ND 2.0**

accommodate every passenger onboard. Ironically, in complying with this safety measure, the boat became even more unsafe, as the extra weight made her more prone to list. Her problems were well known; she'd had a few near misses on Lake Erie and received a warning about the ship's dangerous lack of stability in writing in 1913, yet she sailed on without any additional safety precautions or changes to protocol.

The summer of 1915 had been a cool and damp one, and the *Eastland*'s ticket sales were impacted by the less-than-ideal weather. One of Chicago's largest employers, the Western Electric Company, chartered five ships, including the *Eastland,* to ferry employees and their guests from the Clark Street dock to their employee picnic held at Washington Park in Michigan City, Indiana. There was hope that this voyage would help edge the ship toward profitability during the slow season. The company sold its employees seven thousand tickets to the event at the cost of seventy-five cents each. The *Eastland* was the first of the ships to begin boarding for the journey. Ticket takers were told to load as many passengers as possible onto the *Eastland* to ensure no ticketholders were left behind when the ships set sail. Boarding began at 6:30 in the morning, and soon travelers were entering the ship at a rate of fifty passengers per minute.

The misty weather that morning made the boat's decks slippery, but that did not dampen the sense of excitement in the crowd or prevent people from dancing to the live ragtime music that played from an upper deck. Despite the ship's notorious instability, it was the captain's practice to empty the ballast tanks on the ship to allow the passengers to more easily board the vessel, an undoubtedly welcomed gesture to the women clad in the long, narrow skirts popular during the era and the throngs of children along on the excursion. Many of the passengers were dressed in all white to take part in the parade that would occur when they arrived at the park. With filled picnic baskets, whole families, young sweethearts, and groups of friends were all prepared for a day of summer fun, games, and music.

By seven in the morning, more than one thousand passengers boarded the ship, and people were still streaming into all of the entry-ways unabated. The ship was listing slightly to the port side, but the ticketholders continue to board the ship. By 7:10 in the morning, 2,500 passengers and seventy-five crew members were aboard, and the crew began preparations to bring in the gangplank and start the ship's engines. The ship contained far more people than it was built to carry and more weight than it had ever carried in the past. Orders were sent to fill the ballast tanks to correct the list, and the crew tried to move the passengers from the river-facing port side of the boat to the dock-facing starboard side in an additional effort to correct the list. All of these efforts were unsuccessful, and the list became more pronounced.

The mood of merriment continued on the ship, even as water began to enter the boat through the portside gangways. Within minutes, the list worsened to an estimated twenty-five to thirty degrees of tilt toward the riverside of the vessel. The crew began to realize the boat, now both tipping and filling with water, was in trouble. By 7:28 in the morning, the ship's list was at forty-five degrees, and chaos erupted aboard the *Eastland*. Dishes flew off shelves and crashed to the floor. The refrigerator in the saloon tipped over and slid across the room, pinning two women against the bulkhead. Heavy wooden tables and chairs sailed through rooms, trapping passengers throughout the ship. The piano on the promenade deck skidded the length of the deck, and water began rushing into the portside portholes. Panicked passengers and crew jumped off the starboard side of the ship in an effort to save themselves from the impending calamity.

Within moments, the lines tethering the tilting ship to the dock snapped, tossing passengers and furniture off the ship. Without as much as a splash, the ship quietly rolled into the river on her port side, sinking into twenty feet of murky, polluted water.

Screams of terror coming from all directions filled the air. The bridge and docks were lined with people who could do little but look on in horror as the tragedy unfolded before them. Cries for help came from those flailing in the river, and bystanders on the dock threw anything buoyant they could grab into the river to aid the drowning. The barrage of chicken cages, crates, and other tossed items was meant to be helpful, but the objects hit people struggling to keep their heads above water, sometimes even pushing them below the surface of the sewage-filled water. Desperate people clung to anything within reach, including other passengers. Those who could swim were pulled down by those who couldn't in the urgent bid to grab onto anything that would keep their heads above the foul water. One observer recalled seeing a drowning woman place her baby on a wooden chair floating in the water. She blew a kiss to the baby as she pushed it away from the commotion in the river. The baby sailed away from its mother, then slowly sank beneath the still water. Death seemed to be everywhere.

Inside the boat, hundreds were trapped, some crushed to death under the weight of shifting furniture and the mass of passenger bodies thrust on top of them when the ship tipped over. Others were stuck in cabins and staterooms that were rapidly filling with water. Desperate passengers pounded on the hull of the ship in an attempt to escape before the water that swirled around their knees climbed any further. Witnesses could see the anguished faces of the trapped passengers through the narrow portholes that kept them confined and heard their relentless

"Eastland *Disaster*" *msra images is licensed under CC BY-NC-SA 2.0*

pleas for help as they pounded, scratched, and clawed at the ship that confined them.

Firefighters used axes to hack away at the steel plates on the hull of the ship in an effort to free the living still inside the ship. Nearby steelworkers were pulled away from their jobs and hurried to the boat with their torches; soon, their torches' blue flames were slicing through the hull to reach the living who were frantically trying to escape the ship. Captain Pedersen tried to stop the men from creating holes in his ship, but police intervened, allowing the rescuers to continue despite the raging captain. Rescuers removed passengers by their hair, or anything else they could grab, many emerging with fingers bloodied from clawing at the seams of the boat in the struggle to find means of escape. The luckiest aboard the ship were the passengers on the upper decks of the starboard side of the foundered boat. Those who managed to stay on the ship as it was going down were able to climb over the railing and walk across the hull of the fallen ship toward safety. While the search for the living continued, the dead were being stacked upon the dock.

"Eastland *Disaster*"   *msra images is licensed under CC BY-NC-SA 2.0*

The number of children and young girls who were pulled from the river overwhelmed the crowds of onlookers who gathered in growing numbers on the banks of the river. Each new corpse was met with a wail of despair. As the dead continued to be pulled from the river, a temporary morgue was created inside the Second Regiment Armory to safely store the bodies and allow families to claim their dead. Within hours, forty embalmers and undertakers were working in the unrefrigerated building and would continue to work around the clock for days. Lines of weeping relations snaked around the block, waiting for the opportunity to walk through the rows of bodies and identify the dead. Everything was wet; the bodies oozed river water, which, mixed with the falling rain and the tears of the mourning, saturated everything in the area.

Corpses were lined up in rows of eighty-five, pressed shoulder to shoulder. Some of the drowned mothers laid out were still holding their lifeless infants. Other bodies showed evidence of their final moments of struggle; one woman was brought in with her hands clutching tightly around handfuls of another woman's hair. Witnesses to the gruesome scene later recalled the agony and fear that was shown on the faces of so many of the dead. Marked with nothing but a number, the quickly embalmed bodies waited to be taken home one final time.

The drama of the day was far from over. While the dead were pulled from the river, both the ship's captain and first mate were placed under arrest for negligence. Rescuers were aided by nets that were stretched across the river at Randolph Street to catch the bodies that were pulled from the scene by the current before they were lost to Lake Michigan. To compound the tragedy, the Chicago River was so foul with sewage and pollution that the city, in fear of having a typhoid epidemic, offered free vaccines to anyone, victim or rescuer, who went into the river that day. Despite everything, they continued to raise bodies from the water.

The recovery efforts went on for more than a week. In the end, 844 people died aboard the *Eastland* that day, a number that included just two crew members. Twenty-two entire families were taken by the water. Of the families that lined up for the rare outing, 175 women went home from the dock as widows. Eighty-five men lost their wives in the tragedy, and 290 children died. Seventy percent of those who died in the tragedy were under twenty-five-years old, and the city mourned for the loss of so many young lives.

There was a lack of resources to deal with the overwhelming number of dead. Chicago experienced a shortage of caskets, which delayed a number of funerals. Additionally, there were not enough hearses to transport the dead, so Western Electric Company lent its entire fleet to the cause, and retailer Marshall Field offered delivery trucks to get the victims and their mourners to their final resting places. Gravediggers worked around the clock to prepare graves. The sound of shovels moving through dirt was ceaseless around the Bohemian National Cemetery, the burial site of an estimated one hundred and fifty of *Eastland*'s casualties. In the neighborhoods surrounding Western Electric Company, there were few homes without funeral wreaths on their doors. Mourners went from home to home in a parade of grief, viewing the bodies and paying respects to those lost on the ship. When the

The Eastland *sailing the Great Lakes* **Library of Congress**

funerals began, the processions clogged the streets, and it seemed as if the church bells tolled endlessly in remembrance of the dead.

The desire to determine blame for the loss led to litigation that lasted for nearly twenty years. The captain, some crew, and the ship's owners were all tried on charges of conspiracy to operate an unsafe ship. Defended by the celebrated Clarence Darrow, of Scopes Monkey Trial fame, the group was found not guilty, and not a single person was ever held accountable for the loss of 844 lives. The families of the dead were never compensated by the boat's owners, who, after paying off the ship's debts, were left penniless and went out of business. The tragedy created new safety legislation; most notably stability tests became a standard requirement for ships that sailed the Great Lakes.

Despite the *Eastland*'s tragic history, she sailed again under the new name of the *Wilmette* for the US Navy. The holes in her hull were sealed, then she was converted into a gunboat. The ship was commissioned during both World Wars but never saw action. She served as a training vessel on the Great Lakes and was frequently seen sailing along Chicago's shores. The *Wilmette* was employed by the Navy until she was sold for scrap in 1946.

Today, all that remains are the photos and gravestones of those lost, the memories of those who lived, and the commemorative plaque that was erected on the riverfront in 1989 to honor the catastrophe. The ship is gone, as are all those who lived through that terrible day. The Second Regiment Armory that played such a vital role in the *Eastland* tragedy later became Harpo Studios and was the location of the popular *The Oprah Winfrey Show*. There were countless claims of supernatural experiences in the former makeshift morgue, including glimpses of the spirits of playful children and the sounds of crying, footsteps, and doors opening in unoccupied areas. The most well-known of the rumored apparitions was the Grey Lady, the opaque form of a woman wearing a long dress and an ornate hat who was seen many times and is believed to have been caught on security cameras on more than one occasion. The building was long considered one of Chicago's most haunted locations before it was demolished to make way for new construction in 2016. Despite that all is gone, the story of the *Eastland* continues to be told and is now an integral part of the history of the Great Lakes.

BEWARE THE BREAKERS: *LADY ELGIN* (1851–1860)

The legends and lore surrounding this tragedy make it difficult to definitely know what happened on that stormy September night in 1860. While we will never know how many lives were lost and the wildly conflicting survivor accounts make the events that followed the collision between the *Lady Elgin* and the schooner *Augusta* unclear at best, what is certain is that the event, which left an estimated one thousand Milwaukee children orphaned, began as a party. Spirits were high as the ship set sail from Chicago to Milwaukee at eleven-thirty the night of September 7, 1860. The band played on and on as merrymakers danced and drank beneath the glittering chandeliers of the ship's saloon. The ship was overcrowded, with perhaps as many as five to six hundred people onboard the 252-foot wooden sidewheel steamer, but no one cared while the booze flowed and pretty girls swayed in time to the music.

Estimates of the ship's passengers that night range from just over three hundred people to more than six hundred. While there seems to be little agreement on the number aboard, all agree that the ship was overfilled that night, but when the ship shoved off, few aboard seemed to care. Many of the passengers were part of Milwaukee's recently disarmed Irish Union Guard. Unwilling to support Wisconsin Governor Alexander Randall's secessionist anti-slavery views, the group

The Lady Elgin *sails*   **Wikimedia Commons**

was forcibly disbanded. They'd purchased their one dollar round-trip tickets to the Windy City to see Stephen Douglas and rally support for their Democratic cause. Energized by the events of the day, the group attracted others who wanted to join in on the fun, and many of the revelers followed the Milwaukeeans aboard the ship, where the party continued.

Captain Jack Wilson was at the helm of the *Elgin* that night. Some say he was wary of setting sail that night because he was concerned about the weather, and others dismiss that claim, but all agree he was a well-respected, experienced captain who knew the luxury steamer well. After the ship was safely in open water, Wilson retired to his quarters and went to sleep as the party on the boat continued. The band played on as storm clouds gathered and wind swirled around the ship. As the waves grew, the couples still twirled around the dance floor, paying little mind to the rain that was soon beating against the windows of the saloon.

The celebration lasted into the early hours of the morning. With its gaslights blazing and its running lights gleaming in the inky darkness, the *Elgin* was a bright beacon that stormy night. Also sailing that night was the 128-foot wooden schooner, the *Augusta* (1855–1894). Without her running lights, she was cloaked in darkness and could only be seen when a crack of lightning lit up the stormy skies. The bartenders continued to pour drinks as the dance floor cleared. Tired revelers rested on sofas in the saloon or returned to their cabins to sleep while the band entertained those who were not yet ready to end the night. The party abruptly ended at two-thirty in the morning when the *Elgin* passengers felt a tremendous jolt on the portside of the boat, accompanied by what sounded like an explosion.

Passengers were knocked off sofas and out of their beds by the impact. Chandeliers in the saloon were smashed, sending shards of glass raining down on those on the dance floor. Some accounts claim the impact was so powerful it doused each lamp aboard the ship, plunging the vessel into pitch blackness. Captain Wilson, awakened by the impact, soon discovered that the *Lady Elgin* was rammed amidship by the *Augusta*.

The Augusta *strikes the* Lady Elgin. ***Illustrated for* Frank Leslie's Illustrated Newspaper *in 1860/Wikimedia Commons***

The *Augusta*, sailing low and filled with timber, rushed away from the accident toward Chicago, concerned that she had been so damaged in the collision that her crew was in peril. The crew did not think the *Elgin* was in distress, so they quickly sailed away to save themselves. It was a decision that would be debated for years to come.

Rushing to inspect the damage, Wilson was stunned to see the gaping hole well below the waterline in the side of the *Elgin*. Acting quickly, Wilson ordered the crew to release cargo into the stormy waves in hopes of lightening the ship load to keep her afloat. They released five dozen head of cattle into the water, but it did no good. The crew attempted to fill the hole with mattresses and other materials to slow the sinking of the ship, but the water continued to flow into the hold. Within thirty minutes, the damaged ship would explode, sending splintered pieces of the *Elgin* scattered in the towering waves and untold numbers would be dead.

Those who did not die in the explosion clung to pieces of the ship to keep their heads above the storm-tossed waves. Few made it into one of the three available lifeboats, so the wreckage of the ship was the only salvation available to them. Woven into tales of the survivors is the story of the drummer from the band that played aboard the ship that night safely washing to shore inside of his drum. Another story has survivors climbing on top of an animal pen that was buoyed by the dead cattle inside the pen. Survivors ripped doors from their hinges, pulled themselves up on broken pieces of the hurricane deck, and did anything else they could to keep their heads above water long enough to make it to shore.

Hundreds managed to stay alive to see the beach of Winnetka, Illinois, only to encounter violent breakers and a powerful undertow that dragged many underwater while they were in sight of the rescue they had been praying for since the ship was struck. Those not pulled down by the waves were struck by timbers and other wreckage from the ship that was tossed in the heavy waves. As dawn broke, those in Winnetka witnessed countless dead in the water, each new wave bringing another victim to shore.

It is estimated that just under one hundred people were saved from the wreck on the *Lady Elgin*, many of them returning to Milwaukee the next day by train. The dead washed up on beaches for weeks after the tragedy, making it a grim autumn for those living in the lakeshore communities north of Chicago. Most of the bodies found were sent to Milwaukee's Calvary Cemetery, with many of them remaining unidentified to this day.

For all associated with the *Augusta*, the repercussion of that night continued long after the final recovered victim of the *Elgin* was buried. Milwaukee was in mourning and needed someone to blame for the tragedy, and Captain D. M. Malott was the ideal candidate. Public sentiment was against the man who left the steamer to founder in the storm, and he was eventually arrested and tried for his role in the collision. Later, he was found not guilty of negligence, with the courts finding the blame lay with the law that allowed ships to operate without running lights. This law was eventually changed, but it was too late for the hundreds who perished in the wreck of the *Lady Elgin*.

The ruling did not abate the rage felt for the *Augusta* and her crew. To sidestep the reputation of the boat, her owner painted the hull and changed her name to the *Colonel Cook* in April 1861. These changes did little to disguise her real identity, and when she arrived in Milwaukee that season to pick up a shipment, the boat was surrounded by an angry mob who threatened bodily harm on the crew and to set the former *Augusta* ablaze. The terrified crew fled the city without her load, and the boat was soon sent to the Atlantic Ocean to put distance between the ship and the jeers that met her in the Great Lakes ports. It was during this tumultuous time that the crew quietly began to suspect the ship was now haunted. They reported strange sightings and sounds, which they believed were the spirits of *Lady Elgin* crewmembers who died in the collision. Some even believed the boat was now cursed and destined to sink. The boat's owner dismissed the reports as a combination of rats and drunken delusions, but the sailors disagreed, and the *Cook* became an increasingly uncomfortable ship upon which to work. By 1864, the original *Augusta* crew followed Captain Malott to his new ship, the *Mojave*.

What happens next gives some credence to the rumors that something was amiss after that fateful night in September of 1860. The former *Augusta* eventually sank, wrecking in Lake Erie on September 23, 1894. The ship's new crew survived, but the vessel remained beneath the waves. Its former crew met a similar fate to that of the ship they believed was cursed. Their new ship, the *Mojave*, sank in a storm on November 8, 1864, taking the captain and the crew with her to the bottom of the lake. There were no survivors. The loss of the *Augusta* and her original crew could be looked at as a strange coincidence, or perhaps the stories were true, and the *Lady Elgin* crewmembers did, in the end, issue revenge for what happened on that stormy night on Lake Michigan.

THE UNKNOWN END
OF LYDIA DALE:
J. HAZARD HARTZELL
(1863–1880)

The 130-foot wooden schooner was less than a mile from her destination when she was snared by a storm that would later be known as "The Big Blow." This storm would sink ninety vessels on Lake Michigan and kill 118 sailors before she passed over the lake. It was just after six in the morning on October 16, 1880, when gale-force winds began to swirl around the *J. Hazard Hartzell*. She set sail five days earlier from the L'Anse port in Lake Superior with a load of iron ore bound for Frankfort, Michigan. She neared her destination around three in the morning but decided to drop anchor and sail into the port after daybreak. As the crew battened down the ship's hatches in the rising winds, they grew to regret this decision.

Before long the crew was being pelted with hail and sleet while the waves grew in power and the wind continued to howl. The ship could no longer safely stay anchored in place; the crew pulled up the ship's anchor and attempted to turn her away from the storm. The waves crashed over the deck of the ship as the crew battled against the winds, but the storm was too powerful, and they could not navigate the *Hartzell* to a safer position. Without her anchors, and despite her heavy load, the ship was tossed in the storm. When she was within three hundred yards of the shore, the ship ran aground in a sandbar. Firmly stuck in the sand, the waves relentlessly battered the ship. Finally, she yielded to the attack, and her hull cracked asunder. Within moments, the waves began to tear apart the ship. First it was a single board, then the pieces torn from the ship got gradually larger until all eight crewmembers aboard the *Hartzell* had only one place left to flee the frigid water that was tearing apart the ship: up.

To escape the waves that threatened to sweep them off the ship, the sailors began to climb the ship's riggings to save themselves. It was a crew of eight: seven men and the ship's cook, a woman named Lydia Dale. A plump woman who had spent much of her life in domestic service on land, Dale was unprepared for the nausea-inducing rocking of the ship as it thrashed in the storm. By the time men began to scale the riggings, the cook was so seasick she could no longer stand. Laying on the icy deck under a soaked piece of canvas while pelted by hail, Dale could do nothing but moan in misery. To save the prone woman from being swept off the splintering boat, four men hoisted her up the rigging and tied her weakened body to the mast of the ship. In short order, all aboard the ship were standing on the riggings fifty feet above the deck, and the ship below continued to break apart beneath them.

They had few options as they scanned the horizon, hoping to see a break in the weather or another boat that might render aid. Their salvation came when a young boy walking on the bluff overlooking the lake noticed the ship and the desperate crew clinging to her. He ran home to tell his father, a fisherman who recognized the dangerous position the crew of the *Hartzell* were in. Acting as a town crier, the man rushed to nearby homes and gathered his neighbors, leading them to the bluff to save the stranded crew. Quickly, the group built a bonfire on the beach to get the attention of the *Hartzell*, then used driftwood to spell out the words "lifeboat coming" across the sand. The crew signaled that they received the message, then began to anxiously await their rescue.

Conducting a rescue while the storm raged across the lake would be a dangerous task. Unable to combat the wind and waves in a typical lifeboat, the townspeople knew they needed a rescue cart to reach the boat, but they were without the equipment required for the task. As the winds howled around him and the icy sleet stung his skin, John Woodward climbed upon his horse and rode ten miles north to reach the Point Betsie Lifesaving Station to get what was needed to bring all eight people aboard the ship safely to shore.

Woodward secured the rescue cart that contained a Lyle gun, a short-barreled cannon used to fire a lifeline to stranded boats, a breeches buoy, a life ring attached to a pair of canvas shorts that act like a zipline to transport survivors from a shipwreck to safety, and a surf car, an enclosed vessel used to shuttle more than one person at a time from a wreck. The cart was essential but heavy and difficult to transport along the unpaved pathways that led from the lifesaving station to the shore. Despite the work of twenty-seven men, it took hours of battering through heavy brush, then braving the shifting sands and steep slopes to reach the beach to begin the rescue process. Cold and wet, the men set up the rescue equipment while being pelted by sleet, and the wild winds scoured their exposed skin with swirling sand. The crew clung to

An example of a breeches buoy   **Bain/Wikimedia Commons**

the ship's rigging, eagerly watching the progress and hoping the rescue would come before they were swept into the storm.

It took two shots from the Lyle gun to reach the helpless *Hartzell*. Already covered in ice, the crew onboard worked as quickly as their cold-stiffened hands would allow them to secure the retrieved line so the men on the beach could send over the breeches buoy. While only an estimated three hundred yards from shore, the rescuers fought the heavy waves for seventeen minutes to bring the first man off the boat. When he arrived on the beach, the exhausted first mate could scarcely speak. After a few sips of brandy, the first mate reported there were seven others aboard, including the ship's cook, Lydia Dale, who was unwell. When asked why the woman was not immediately sent from the ship, as was the long-held custom of providing lifesaving aid to women and children first, he stated that Dale would not use the immodest breeches buoy. In response, the villagers quickly readied the surf car to be sent to the storm-tossed ship to retrieve the woman.

Squinting through the sheets of sleet while they laboriously pulled the surf car through the stormy waters, they could see little of what was happening on the sinking ship. After the car skidded to a stop on the windswept beach, the rescuers were surprised when they opened the car's door to discover two ice-encrusted men inside rather than the expected Lydia Dale. The sailors assured them Dale would be the next to leave the ship, and so they again sent the car into the heavy waves toward the *Hartzell*.

On the surf car's second trip to the foundering ship, it was the captain and the second mate who arrived on the beach. The villagers' confusion grew to anger when it was realized that Dale was still aboard the *Hartzell*. The rescuers had been on the beach for hours being lashed by the storm, and their patience with the crew who would save themselves before the ailing Lydia Dale was wearing thin. The captain assured the villagers that Dale was certain to arrive in the next surf car trip.

The sun was growing ever lower in the sky as the villagers, now grumbling about the "cowardly" *Hartzell* crew, sent the cart out once more to the ship. From the beach, they watched the ship's mast sway wildly in the wind, and they feared it would topple before they reached the three remaining crewmembers. When the now dented and battered surf car was pulled from the waves, the sun had set. As the car door opened on the darkened beach, it took a few moments for the villagers to realize the car contained the two remaining crewmen. There was no sign of Lydia Dale, who was last seen tied to the mast of the ship and unable to climb down on her own. The crowd on the beach erupted into angry jeers at the sailors, while others lamented the day spent battling a storm to rescue the kind of men who would abandon a woman on a sinking ship.

The last men to arrive on the beach attempted to convince the crowd that Dale was dead and had been for hours as rigor mortis had already overtaken her body. The rescuers were skeptical of these claims, wondering why her death had not been mentioned earlier. It was now too dark to send the surf car on another run into the storm. There would be no further attempts to reach the ship that night. Reluctantly, the rescuers left the beach, fearful they left a living woman still tied to the mast of the sinking ship but unable to rescue her if they did.

At dawn, some of the townsmen returned to the beach, but the mast of the *Hartzell* was gone. The remaining rigging had been pulled down into the waves, and there was no trace of where the *J. Hazard Hartzell* ran aground. The rescued crew quickly left town, and all that remained of them was the uneasy feeling that something unsettling happened aboard the lost ship.

An answer to the nagging question many had about the fate of the woman left aboard the ship came seventeen days later. Lydia Dale's body washed up on the beach where the townspeople had spent all day trying to rescue her. An autopsy determined that the woman died not of exposure, or illness, but of drowning. The results sent a shockwave through the small town, as many believed the report was evidence that the woman was left alive on the wreck and drowned when the mast upon which she was tied was pulled down into the waves. What really happened to the cook will forever remain a mystery. Whether she was abandoned by the crew because they found it too difficult to hoist her down from the riggings or if they mistakenly believed she was dead will never be revealed. The truth of the death of Lydia Dale disappeared under Lake Michigan's waves the moment the mast of the *J. Hazard Hartzell* was toppled by the storm.

AN ETERNAL CRY
FOR HELP: *IRONSIDES*
(1864–1873)

It started as a rumor in the ports along Lake Michigan. Weathered sailors gathered in shipyards, sharing their stories with anyone who would listen. These men were certain that the wreck of *Ironsides* was no accident, and they wanted the boat's owners to be held accountable for the unnecessary loss of twenty lives.

Ironsides, a 218-foot wooden steamer, was designed to transport both passengers and cargo on the Great Lakes. When she launched in 1864, she was celebrated for the unparalleled luxury and elegance she offered riders. Marketing materials boasted of her "Brussels carpet," damask curtains, and the twinkling chandeliers in the cabins. Those who booked passage in one of her forty-four staterooms enjoyed the added extravagance of marble bath fixtures and hot and cold running water in the rooms, something many homes of the day did not have. The boat, with her gleaming wood and her attentive crew, offered riders the finest comforts that could be had on the Lakes.

While the exterior of the ship dazzled passengers, the crew knew the truth behind the facade. The sailors were aware the ship was leaky and noticed that each time they would unload the cargo hold, the cargo being transported was even wetter than it had been on its last journey. Rumors circulated among the mariners that she was unseaworthy and that the company was willing to pay the crew more than the going rate to sail on the increasingly dangerous ship, rather than making the needed repairs. The sailors believed she required a complete overhaul, but the Milwaukee-based Englemann Transportation Company that owned her disagreed. They added a few coats of paint and some replaced boards, and that was all that was needed for her to pass her inspection and be declared in "excellent shape" during the winter of 1872–1873. Despite the glowing review, in less than a year, she'd be permanently at rest beneath Lake Michigan's waves.

On what was to be her final journey, she left Milwaukee shortly before ten in the evening on her way to Grand Haven, Michigan, with a partially loaded cargo hold. Onboard were nineteen passengers and thirty crewmen. The September winds were mild on both sides of the lake when she set sail, but just after midnight, gale winds swirled around the boat, and soon she was battling a storm. The heavy waves and howling winds punished the boat. As she twisted in the waves in a fight to stay afloat, cracks appeared in her body, and the leaks in the boat rapidly multiplied. Water rushed in from each new break in the steamer. To combat the flooding, the ship's pumps ran for hours without ceasing, but they were no match for the streams of water that flowed from every fault in the battered ship. By seven in the morning, the water was knee-deep in the belly of the boat, and it was still rising.

The relentless waves continued to pummel the ship, smashing through the gangway door. At nine in the morning, the crew raised the *Ironsides'* distress flag as the boat continued to fill with water. Despite the pumps and the crew's frantic bailing of the ship, eventually the engine flooded and the ship lost power, making her impossible to move. With little hope of being aided by another ship in the midst of the violent storm and no possibility of making it to the harbor in the *Ironsides*, the crew quickly distributed life preservers and readied the passengers for the inevitable sinking of the ship.

By eleven in the morning, all passengers and crew were wearing flotation devices and aboard one of the five lifeboats. The storm continued to rage, and the gale winds tossed the lightweight crafts through the twelve-foot waves. As the boats battled through the water, a few of its occupants were thrown from the boats and into the stormy waters. Those who remained in the boats fared little better than those flung into the waves. Outmatched by the storm, three of the five lifeboats soon capsized, leaving all inside to the merciless lake. Only two of the lifeboats made it to shore. In total, twenty souls were drowned in their pursuit of land.

When the storm dissipated, a few of the remaining crew who survived the perilous storm guided rescue boats to the site of the sinking, in hopes of recovering additional survivors. Sadly, none were to be found. The lifeless bodies of the passengers bobbed in the waves near the spot where the *Ironsides* sank; they were dragged from the waves, and the corpses were then placed in wooden boxes for their return journeys to Milwaukee. A water-logged body of a young mother who boarded in Milwaukee with her four-year-old son was retrieved from the lake and placed in a box large enough to accommodate her and her son. The golden-haired boy, clad in a blue sailor suit, was not with the other dead, drifting in the current. Reluctant to leave the child unrecovered, the men continued to search for the small body.

After an extensive search, the boy was discovered, half buried in the sand. When he was freed, his appearance stunned the recovery team. Instead of being battered in the storm, his delicate skin was unmarred by the tragedy. His face looked placid, almost as if he were sleeping, and he was described by the recovery team as appearing as ethereal when he was placed in the box next to his mother. In the days that followed, debated raged over the seaworthiness of the ship and who bore responsibility for the deaths of those drowned in the storm, but in the end the bluster that briefly made national news ended with little impact on the owners of the boat or the surviving crew.

This should have been the end of the story of the *Ironsides*, but its story continues to this day. There is a persistent belief that the ship's youngest passenger, whose life ended during the storm, somehow lives on. Those who believe the ghost of Henry Valentine, the boy who drowned in 1873, continues to linger in the area got all the proof they needed that his spirit remains in the lake on August 6, 2000, the final day of the annual Grand Haven Coast Guard Festival in Grand Haven, Michigan. On that day, the USCG vessel the *Mackinaw*, a 290-foot ice-breaker, was sailing through heavy fog when the crew on the deck heard the distinct sounds of a child calling for help. When the sailors could not locate the child in distress, they contacted the Grand Haven Coast Guard station, who quickly sent a rescue boat to search for the child.

When the deployed rescue boat joined the icebreaker, both boats could hear the child in distress calling for help from the unseen depths of the fog. Their search was intense but proved fruitless. Unwilling to leave a child in peril, the crew contacted nearby pleasure boats to see if help was needed, but the cries had not come from any of the nearby ships. Next, local law enforcement was contacted to see if anything had been reported, but there had been no accidents and no calls for aid. The crews on both boats were baffled and perplexed. They needed an explanation for the cries they heard and reassurance that there was not a child in danger who needed their help. Despite the teams diligently scouring the area, no one in distress was ever discovered.

Later, when discussing the mysterious cries for help, it was noted the *Mackinaw* was sailing over the sunken remains of the *Ironsides* when the cries were heard. Could the Coast Guard crews have detected the call for help that has been sounding since the awful storm that took the *Ironsides*, as well as Henry Valentine, his mother, and eighteen others, in 1873? For some, the answer to this question is an emphatic yes, and this strange tale is offered as proof that the boy continues to wait for the rescue that did not reach him in time all those years ago.

THE LEGENDARY CHRISTMAS TREE BOAT: *ROUSE SIMMONS* (1868–1912)

The *Rouse Simmons* was a three-mast wooden schooner built in Milwaukee and launched on August 27, 1868. The wooden-hulled working ship spent most of her life hauling lumber. By the fall of 1912, the forty-four-year-old ship had seen better days. She could still hold her three-to-four-hundred-ton capacity, but she was leaky, and her captain had skipped the last round of badly needed caulking that only made the leaking worse.

The ship's captain, and one-eighth owner of the boat, was the Algoma born Herman Schuenemann who had spent most of his life on Lake Michigan. Sailing since childhood, he had worked the last three decades of his life hauling Christmas trees on the lake. In Chicago, where he lived with his wife and three daughters, he was affectionally known as Captain Santa, selling his evergreen trees from a dock off the Clark Street Bridge to German immigrants during the holidays. The cost of the trees varied from a few quarters to a dollar, but the kind captain could always be relied upon to generously supply free trees to needy families and orphanages. Gifting trees to those who could not otherwise decorate for the season made him a well-known, and well-loved, man on the wharf.

In November of 1912, the ship was scheduled to leave Chicago, bound for northern Michigan and a load of the coveted Christmas trees. November is a notoriously difficult month on the Great Lakes, and its gales sometimes blow with the ferocity of a hurricane. Schuenemann did not need to be reminded of the danger of the fierce autumn storms; his brother died in a November gale on the way back from a tree run in 1899.

From the onset, there were difficulties with the planned journey. Co-captain and partial owner of the ship Captain Nelson had grown wary of the aged boat. When discussing the voyage, he confided in his sister that he doubted the *Rouse Simmons'* seaworthiness, but he felt he needed to make the last run of the season to honor his commitment to Schuenemann. Nelson's daughter, Alvida, begged her father not to set sail with the boat. Many believe her tearful pleading was related to a premonition she had about the fate of that final journey of the year. Despite young Alvida's tears and his own misgivings, Nelson made the voyage, promising his family it would be his final tree run on the *Rouse Simmons*. It was later discovered that Schuenemann made the same promise to his own family.

The schooner was scheduled to leave Chicago on a Friday, an unlucky day in the eyes of many superstitious mariners. Crews have been known to wait to set sail until one minute after midnight in order to avoid the cursed day. Further alarm sounded when it was noted there were an unlucky thirteen men on the roster for the journey. Despite the compounded bad luck, the captains pressed on. As the crew loaded on the boat, they noticed that rats were exiting the ship in large numbers. Sailors know that rats fleeing a ship is a bad sign. Rats are great harbingers of danger, as they wriggle into the tightest of areas, and are the first to find leaks and other evidence that the ship was taking on water. As the exodus was observed, the moods of the men further darkened. Even with their mounting concerns, the crew boarded and set sail for the northern woods.

The journey to Michigan was an uneventful one, but then when they reached the shore, the crew again noticed another parade of rats fleeing

The wooden schooner Rouse Simmons *before she sank*   ***Alpena Co. George N. Fletcher Public Library***

the ship. Eager to reload the schooner and take advantage of the calm waters, the captains ignored the crew's reports. The men worked feverishly to load the ship with evergreens. Once the sailors filled the cargo hold with trees, they began to stack the decks with towering mounds of trees. When completed, the men hauled 5,500 trees aboard, and some described the stocked *Rouse Simmons* as looking like a floating forest.

   With the ship loaded and ready to set sail, some of the crew hesitated before reboarding. The ship appeared to be dangerously overloaded, and the threat of an incoming storm was in the air. If the sailors did not return with the ship, they would forego all pay they had earned, as the men were only paid when the journey was completed. Many men were unable to afford the lost wages and the expense to return home if they abandoned the journey so they reluctantly reboarded the schooner. A few men, heeding the warning of the fleeing rats, elected to return to Chicago by rail. The captains, seeing an additional opportunity to make money, sold the spots vacated by the wary crew to lumberjacks seeking a ride to Chicago.

While the exact number is not known, when the loaded ship left the docks, it may have had anywhere between sixteen and twenty-three souls on board. The *Rouse Simmons* set sail when the skies were clear and the waves calm, but before long, they ran into heavy weather. The beleaguered men had no idea they were about to encounter what would later be called "the greatest storm of the decade." Soon, the men were battling 65-mile-per-hour winds that came with a cold rain that soaked them to the bone as they struggled to keep the schooner afloat. The situation became dire when the temperature dropped, and before long the rain turned to wet, heavy snow that clung to the ship. The men fought forty-foot waves as walls of water crashed upon the deck of the ship. Soon, the boat, and the men, were coated in a shell of ice.

As the desperate *Rouse Simmons* neared Kewaskum, Wisconsin, she sent a distress signal. The struggling boat could be seen from shore, her sails torn and her deck weighted down by ice. A gas-powered lifeboat was dispatched to aid the disabled ship. The rescue crew motored to the failing ship, keeping her in their eyeline. Without warning, a snow squall swooped into the area, reducing the visibility in the lifeboat to zero. They estimated they were within one thousand yards of the ship before they lost sight of her. When the storm cleared, the *Rouse Simmons* had vanished without a trace. The stunned rescue crew returned to the shore, alone.

The boat and her crew had disappeared, but traces of the ship continued to appear on Lake Michigan shores. Shortly after the boat sank, a message in a bottle, sealed with a piece of pinewood, washed up in Sheboygan. The note, thought to have been written by Captain Nelson, reads as follows:

> Friday . . . everyone goodbye. I guess we are all through. During the night the small boat washed overboard. Leaking bad. Invald and Steve lost too. God help us.

Beyond that message, the only evidence the ship had ever been there were the evergreens that continued to wash ashore. The green trees, ready for Christmas decorations, were claimed by the townspeople who joked that Captain Santa continued his job of delivering trees. When the pines that washed up to shore were no longer green, the townspeople used the wood to create Christmas ornaments.

Interest in the ship was renewed in 1924 when Captain Schuenemann's wallet was recovered from the lake. The wallet, made of waterproof oilskin, remained watertight, and the undamaged contents of the pouch were returned to the man's widow. As the story was relayed, it was noted with a twinkle in the storyteller's eye that the name of the fishing boat that recovered Captain Santa's wallet was *Reindeer*.

No further trace of the ship was discovered until 1971. A diver found the wreckage of the mysteriously missing ship fifty-nine years after she vanished off the coast of Two Rivers. It was then observed she lost her steering wheel, making it impossible for the crew to sail to the safety of the shore. The diver also noted the good luck horseshoe found on many boats that hung from the cabin wall near the steering wheel was missing one of its nails. Rather than being in the upside-down, u-shaped position that allows the horseshoe to "gather luck," as if in a bucket, the shoe was facing downward; all of its luck had, indeed, run out.

The dive might have helped to solve the mystery of what happened to this ship, but legend still clings to this boat. Thirteen days after the *Rouse Simmons* went down, sailors on the lake claimed to hear the phantom tolling of the schooner's bell. Traditionally, the bell is tolled to note the loss of life, and men on the lake were convinced the ship was tolling for its own death and the death of its crew.

To this day, people still claim to see the *Rouse Simmons* sailing on moonlit nights. The sightings increase as the calendar nears closer to Christmas. Those who see the ship report that her sails are ripped to tatters and they are wildly flapping in the wind, as if they are under attack from gale-force winds, even on the calmest of nights. Observers watch her sail, and soon she disappears into the mist, once again gone from view.

True to the legend, the lake does not give up her dead, and the Christmas Tree boat was not an exception; no bodies have ever been recovered from the wreck. The widow Schuenemann continued the Christmas tree business as best she could without her husband but eventually retired. The wife of Captain Santa died in 1933 and is buried at the Arcadia Park Cemetery in Chicago. Next to her tombstone is a simple stone acknowledging her husband, with an evergreen etched into the monument. It is said that those who visit the gravesite are met with the overwhelming scent of evergreens, despite there being no pine trees in the area.

LAKE ONTARIO

Lake Ontario, the most easterly of the Great Lakes, has a surface area of 7,340 miles. While similar in size to Lake Erie, Ontario is much deeper, holding nearly four times the water found in Erie. With an average depth of 283 feet, at its deepest, the lake measures a depth of 802 feet. Supplying fresh drinking water to nine million people, Lake Ontario is the fourteenth largest lake in the world. Some say the name "Ontario" is derived from the Iroquoian language, meaning "lakes of shining waters," while others believe its origin is in the Huron word for "great lake." In either case, the lake has played an essential role in the development of transportation and trade in North America.

All of the Great Lakes flow into Lake Ontario, causing it to be the most polluted of the five Lakes. Its primary inlet is Niagara Falls, and its primary outlet is the Saint Lawrence River. The first lake in the Saint Lawrence Seaway, it is the gateway to the Atlantic Ocean and a critical pathway for international trade and transportation. Since white settlers began to explore the area in the early 1600s, the lake has played a key role in European expansion and the development of the United States and Canada.

At varying points in history, the Canadian, English, French, United States, and First Nations have all had a military presence on Lake Ontario. The lake played a critical role in the French Indian Wars (1754–1763), American Revolutionary War (1775–1783), and the War of 1812 (1812–1815). Most of the oldest shipwrecks found beneath Ontario's waves are connected to this early military maneuvering. While it is unknown how many shipwrecks have occurred on the lake, an estimated two hundred have been identified, and the search is ongoing. The pollution from the western Lakes, coupled with invasive species, like zebra mussels, brought in on vessels from the Atlantic have made preserving Lake Ontario shipwrecks a challenge. Today there are a number of non-profit organizations working to preserve the history that rests on the deep lake's floor.

Lake Serpent

The Seneca people called it *Gaasyendietha*, a serpentine, dragon-like creature who could breathe fire and fly and was said to live in Lake Ontario. Early fur trappers told tales of a long serpent who slithered through the lake at great speeds, occasionally leaping from the water to its massive form. As the culture around the lake changed, the sightings of a mysterious beast continued. In an 1829 newspaper account from the area now known as St. Catharines, children spotted a "hideous water serpent" while playing on the beach. Thirteen years later, the creature appeared near that beach again, witnesses saying it was between thirty and forty feet long and brown with a large head.

It wasn't just children who reported seeing the unidentified animal; in 1833 a schooner captain and his crew reported seeing a 175-foot blue serpent slink past their boat and glide toward the St. Lawrence River. A fisherman in 1877 reported he'd seen something that looked like "a log with [a] mouth like a crocodile," and offered his oar with the beast's toothmarks on it as evidence of the sighting. Not to be outdone, in 1882, a fifty-foot-long lake serpent was spotted near Toronto. Said to be as wide as a man and colored a bluish grey, this beast had the distinction of being covered in stiff bristles. While these tales of a creature lurking in the lake are often retold, there have been few modern sightings of the serpent.

THE ELUSIVE HISTORIC TREASURE: HMS *ONTARIO* (1780–1780)

L ittle is known about the final journey of the HMS *Ontario*, but for years she was among the most sought-after sunken vessels on the Great Lakes. Often called the "Holy Grail of Shipwrecks" by Great Lakes divers, the twenty-two cannon, eighty-foot brig sloop was the largest and most powerful British warship on the Lakes when she was launched on May 10, 1780. Built to battle the rebelling colonists in the American Revolutionary War, in its early days of use, she ferried troops and supplies to the upper New York State military bases.

In October of 1780, the ship set sail at Fort Niagara with a final destination of Fort Haldimand. While the official records indicate the ship carried seventy-four military personnel, nine women and children, four Native American guides, and one civilian, many historians believe the ship went down with an estimated 130 or more people on board. Private correspondence regarding the ship indicates that the ship could have had as many as 120 people sailing, as well as an additional thirty American prisoners of war.

While on the water, the warship was caught in a storm created by the epic Hurricane of 1780. Originating in the Caribbean and considered to be one of the deadliest storms in history, the destructive weather pattern took an estimated 22,000 lives. By the time the storm reached New England, it had become a powerful Nor'easter, and it likely left the ship battling 60- to 90-mile-per-hour winds. Nothing is known of what happened to the *Ontario* when she met the storm, but it is believed she sunk on October 31, 1780.

Days after the sinking, a few items from the ship washed ashore: blankets, a few hats, and compass parts but no large pieces of the ship, or traces of those who were on board. The British conducted an extensive search in the days that followed, but all that was recovered were the sails from the missing ship. News of the missing ship was kept quiet, as the British were eager to hide their military loss from General Washington and his troops.

The Royal Navy warship was rediscovered on the US–Canadian border in 2008 by a pair of expert divers. This ship, which never saw a battle and only sailed for five months, finally made history when found by being both the oldest wreck ever found on the Great Lakes and the oldest fully intact warship of its kind that still exists in the world. Miraculously, the centuries-old ship is beautifully preserved, even retaining some of her original glass windowpanes. She lays five hundred feet beneath the surface of the water and is thought to be so intact because she is at a depth where little sunlight or oxygen can get to the ship to accelerate the process of decay. Despite being at depths that cannot be reached by recreational divers, the exact location of this wreck remains undisclosed to protect this unique piece of history. The wreck, considered to be a British war grave, belongs to the United Kingdom, and there are no plans to raise her from the icy depths of the lake that shares her name.

THE LEGEND ENDURES: HMS *SPEEDY* (1798–1804)

The impact of the 1804 sinking of the HMS *Speedy* is still being felt today. History lovers cite the impact the sinking had on the development of the Canadian government. Mystery fans are intrigued by the search for the still-missing ship, and seekers of the supernatural are enthralled with folklore woven into this captivating tale.

Mounting tensions between the newly formed United States and Britain, which eventually led to the War of 1812, prompted the hasty construction of the *Speedy*. While she was designed for war, she spent much of her time on the Lakes acting as a ferry. The two-mast, eighty-foot gunboat was constructed of green timber, which caused the ship to suffer from dry rot and leaking soon after she made her debut on Lake Ontario. In the weeks before what would be her final journey, she sat in the harbor, leaking so badly that she required daily bailing to keep the rotting vessel above the waves.

The tale of her final journey begins months earlier in an upper-Canadian fur camp. The indigenous Anishinabek people and the white trappers and traders who moved onto their lands struggled through occasional clashes. The Farewell brothers brought John Sharpe into their trading camp, and soon after, Sharpe slayed an indigenous man in an altercation. The dead man's family agreed to let the English govern-ment punish Sharpe for the murder. Time passed, and Sharpe remained a free man, so eventually it became clear that there would be no consequences for the white man who took an indigenous life. Enraged, the dead man's brother, Ogetonicut, sought to even the score between Sharpe and his family and visited the man. Gripping a club, Ogetonicut denounced the man, then struck him in the head several times until Sharpe lay dead with a hole in his skull.

Ogetonicut did nothing to conceal the dispensation of what he believed to be justice, and shortly after, he was arrested by the English authorities. The Anishinabek balked at the uneven enforcement of English laws, but they were powerless to stop the government from taking Ogetonicut away in shackles. His guilt was a foregone conclusion, and soon plans were underway for both his trial, and the eventual hanging that would follow.

The territory was ruled by English law, which dictated that crimes must be tried where they are committed. As yet, no place had been established in this region to conduct business of the state. The necessity for a trial in the region excited many white men who aspired to establish a government center in Newcastle on Presqu'ile Point. This official trial and execution would be the ideal way to make Newcastle the region's center. Once the arrangements had been made, the HMS *Speedy* was loaded with those who would participate in the trial. On board were the trial judge, Ontario's first solicitor-general, government officials, police officers, trial witnesses, the manacled defendant, and his attorney, Scotsman Angus McDonnell, among others. It is lost to history exactly how many people boarded the leaky boat on October 7, 1804, but it is believed to be between twenty and thirty-nine people, including two children whose parents were witnesses in the trial but journeyed by foot as an expense saving measure.

Captain Paxton, aware of the ship's troubles, was reluctant to set sail but was ordered to do so or risk being court-martialed by one of the dignitaries sailing to the trial. Before she left the port, she ran aground, but that did not lessen the demands on Paxton to make the hundred-mile journey from York to Newcastle on the overtaxed boat. The boat stopped at a nearby port to pick up the Farewell brothers, who were key witnesses in the trial. The men appraised the boat, riding low in the water and containing an air of rot, and refused to board, opting instead to follow the *Speedy* by canoe. The brothers were able to stay in sight of the *Speedy* on the first leg of their journey.

The next day, the winds rose, and the *Speedy* was caught in the midst of a snow squall. The gale-force winds churned the waves and tossed the boat mercilessly. The ship tried to sail for safe harbor, but she couldn't battle the winds. In the storm, the canoers lost sight of the *Speedy* as they made their way to the shelter of the shore. The *Speedy* searched for shelter while snow and the growing darkness made sight navigation impossible. In an act of desperation, the ship fired its cannon in the storm to signal the ship was in trouble. In response to the call for help, those onshore quickly lit bonfires to draw the *Speedy* safely in, but as they fed the flames, they never saw the ship on the horizon. The *Speedy* went down in the waves with no survivors and no trace of where she went.

According to lore, it was not just the unseaworthy boat and bad weather that doomed the journey. Generations of storytellers have indicated there was something greater at work. In many versions of the story, Ogetonicut is accompanied on board by a tribal elder. The man, who had been plagued by a lifetime of dreams that showed him dying aboard an English boat, sensed the HMS *Speedy* was the boat that had been haunting his dreams for years the moment he stepped aboard. Knowing his fate had long ago been sealed, he calmly boarded, assured the white men who acted unjustly against the Anishinabek would meet the same fate. It is also said that Ogetonicut's mother, aware she would lose a second son to the white settlers, enacted her own version of justice. Legend holds that the grieving mother enacted a sacred dance atop of Scarborough Bluffs as the ship passed, cursing the ship and all aboard.

Adding to the mysticism surrounding the sinking of the ship, there are some that believe the Sophiasburgh Triangle, thought to be located on the western end of Prince Edward County at the entrance to Presqu'ile Bay, played a role in the tragedy. The infamous area is said to have its own magnetic field, causing compasses to give incorrect readings. It is said the area can cause a compass discrepancy of up to twenty degrees.

The wreck shaped Upper Canada's future. The ship disappeared with key members of the Canadian government and, if rumors are to be believed, some early copies of the emerging Canadian constitution. After the loss of the *Speedy*, Newcastle was deemed too difficult to reach, so the government center was moved to the city now called Cobourg. The wreck also spawned a mystery that endures more than two hundred years after the boat vanished.

Historians and divers have been searching for the *Speedy* for years. She remains missing to this day, at least officially. Over the years a number of people have claimed to have discovered her, yet none have been definitively proven to be the elusive ship. Many believe the ship struck a limestone rock formation once known as the Devil's Horseback. The formation, which appeared on navigation charts at the time, inexplicably disappeared from the lake, leading some to believe the ship struck the rock formation with enough force to topple it and destroy the rotting vessel. The most recent claim of discovery was made by Ed Burtt, who added the tantalizing detail that he spotted a pair of moccasins next to a jailer's chain aboard the wreck he discovered. His wreck, and the many others also suspected to be the *Speedy*, remain well beneath the waves of Ontario's cold waters, waiting for an ending to this tale.

THE MYSTERIOUS DISAPPEARANCE OF THE MASONIC SKIPPER: *GEORGE A. MARSH* (1882–1917)

John Wesley Smith, the skipper of the ill-fated *George A. Marsh*, is a man who died twice. He was declared dead with eleven others, including seven children, when his schooner loaded with coal foundered during a storm on August 8, 1917. Ten years later, he was interred in an Oklahoma cemetery after he died of natural causes. How Smith made it from the stormy waters of Lake Ontario to the dusty streets of Harrah, Oklahoma, remains a mystery to this day.

With Smith at the helm, the *George A. Marsh* set sail from Oswego, New York, filled with a load of coal to be delivered to Kingston, Ontario. On board was Smith's wife and five of his children, his brother, William, as well as First Mate William Watkins, deckhand George Cousins, along with deckhand Neil McClennan, his wife, infant child, and young nephew. When the wooden, three-mast ship set sail, the summer day was clear and breezy. Three hours into her journey, the boat met a sudden storm. Thirty-five-mile-per-hour winds blew the lake into a frenzy. Powerful waves crashed again and again over the decks, and by five in the evening, the *Marsh* was battling both a storm and a leak.

The onboard pumps could not keep up with the leak, and the ship filled with water faster than she could be cleared. The additional weight of the water caused her to ride increasingly lower in the waves. With the storm still tearing across the lake, Smith determined the group's best hope for survival would be to beach the embattled ship on nearby Pigeon Shoal, which would allow all aboard to wait for rescue without fear of drowning. After a night of fighting the storm, in the early morning hours, the ship suddenly rolled over, forcing all fourteen people aboard into the water. One lifeboat had been set afloat, and inside were William Smith and Neil McClennan, who clutched Smith's baby to his chest as the yawl rowed away from the storm. Clinging to the side of the yawl was twelve-year-old Greta Smith, who struggled to keep her head above the waves. She held on tightly in a desperate bid to survive, but the powerful storm and cold water took their toll on the girl. Before long, her strength failed, and she slipped beneath the water, never to be seen again.

In the distance, the lighthouse keeper on Simcoe Island saw the ship fail but could not safely reach the ship to offer aid, due to the storm. Through the rough waters and the blackness of the night, the two men rowed towards Amherst Island. The next morning, they were rescued by fisherman Benjamin Wemp, who found the men cold and exhausted, with McClennan still clinging to Smith's daughter, who had died in the night due to exposure. It was only then the men realized they were the only ones who survived the sinking of the *George A. Marsh*. When word spread of the sinking, local sailors were sympathetic regarding the loss of life but were critical of the decisions that led to the tragedy. Many thought the boat, and the sailors on board, were past their prime and bringing children aboard was dangerous folly. A mariner was quoted by the *Toronto Globe* as saying:

> A lake schooner in these days, when all of them are long past
> their prime, is no place for women and children. An ordinary
> crew with ordinary luck may get away in a shipwreck, but a
> sixteen foot yawl boat, even in smooth water would be crowded

with fourteen persons, and in a sea running Wednesday morning, it would be impossible to keep the best of yawl boats right side up.

The town of Belleville, Ontario, grieved for the death of those lost on the *George A. Marsh*. A memorial for all twelve of the victims was presented at St. Thomas' Anglican Church, the home congregation to many of the lost. The well-attended service honored the lives of Smith, his twenty-two-year-old second wife, and his children Greta, Eva, John, Clarence, and baby Lorraine. McClellan said goodbye to his twenty-five-year-old wife, infant son Douglas, and his four-year-old nephew George "Buster" Greaves. Also honored were sixty-six-year-old crewmen Watkins, and Cousins, aged fifty-nine. Candles were burned, and hymns were sung, but the families did not have the comfort of laying their dead to rest, as none of the dead had yet to be recovered.

Slowly, the lake began to give up the bodies. On August 14, a group of boys taking photographs of the wreck found the badly decomposed body of Cousins in three feet of water in the shoals near Amherst Island. On August 20, the body of a woman washed ashore near Lake Ontario Park, but the disfigured corpse could not be positively identified as either Mrs. Smith or Mrs. McClellan. Wharf favorite, young Buster, was also recovered in the days that followed, but the remaining bodies were lost to the lake.

After sinking, the boat lay at the bottom of the lake under eighty feet of water, with her masts rising from the waves. In the fall of 1917, her masts were removed to eliminate hazards to any other ship, and that may have been the end of the story of the schooner had a letter not been sent to Margaret Smith in March of 1927.

In 1917, then sixteen-year-old Margaret Smith and her fourteen-year-old brother Horace were left orphaned after the sinking of the *Marsh*. Shortly after the accident, Margaret married the newly widowed Neil McClellan, and the newly formed family moved forward in the wake of the tragedy. For ten years, all had assumed that Smith drowned in the wreck, but Master Ben Wilson of the Harrah, Oklahoma Free and Accepted Masons had news that would shatter this belief. Wilson, who was asked by his Masonic brother Smith to contact his previous lodge upon his death, started a new life after the accident. Arriving in Oklahoma without means, Wilson helped the former sailor become established in this landlocked town more than two thousand miles from his home in Belleville. Through hard work, Smith became a successful business owner. As his life came to a close, he confided in his friend Wilson of his long-held secret, telling him of the accident, the loss of his family, and that he was presumed dead. As a final act, he left all of his possessions to his two living children he abandoned after the wreck. Sworn to secrecy, Wilson notified the Lodge and the Smith children upon John Smith's February 22, 1927 death.

Shock and disbelief soon gave way to acceptance, and by early March, the news had spread all over Smith's former hometown. Horace readily believed Smith was his father, recalling that the man was an excellent swimmer, and it was possible for him to have gotten to Amherst Island after the boat went down. Margaret questioned Wilson regarding the appearance of the man who claimed to be her father and surmised that the lodge brother was likely her father. McClellan, who survived that terrible night on the lake, speculated that Smith may have fled to escape the consequences of the wreck and to avoid the questions as to why he lived when the rest of his family died. Smith's estate, worth $3,000 in 1927 (an estimated contemporary value of $45,000), was awarded to his children. His body remains buried in Oklahoma, far away from the family plot of the other Smiths who called him husband and father in his lifetime.

The layers of intrigue surrounding the events of August 8, 1917, do not end with the mysterious actions of Smith. Rumors dating back decades traveled around the lake that there was a chest of riches in the shallow water near Sodus, New York. News of Smith's escape from death reignited the tales of hidden treasure. The son of the captain of the *City of Dresden* recalled a conversation between his father and Smith the day the *George A. Marsh* vanished. In hushed tones, the men discussed retrieving the treasure and splitting the bounty. Hours later, the schooner set sail, and the ship went down, and neither the ship nor Smith were ever seen again. After it was discovered that Smith survived the wreck, a new story began to emerge that the chest was on the ship when it foundered and the treasure was inside the submerged schooner. Small regional newspapers revived the legend of the chest of riches, some even reprinting maps of the lake that showed where the *George A. Marsh* sank, introducing the intriguing tale to a whole new generation of fortune-seekers.

The final resting place of the boat is as unusual as the tales that surround her. The *George A. Marsh* foundered in an area known as the Marysburgh Vortex. Considered to be the "Bermuda Triangle of Lake Ontario," the area, which spans from Prince Edward County east to the Saint Lawrence River and then north to Kingston, has been associated with a number of shipwrecks and missing boats, as well as downed planes and some otherworldly experiences. Claims of lake monsters, mermaids, and UFO sightings have all been made in areas inside the vortex. The story of the *George A. Marsh*, with its disappearing skipper and its rumor of riches, fits in well with the tales of mysterious fogs, magnetic abnormalities, and other strange tales from the fabled location.

GONE IN A FLASH:
JOHN B. KING
(1863–1930)

It had been a hot stretch of days in late June when two ladies sat fanning themselves on the veranda of the Walklete summer cottage. The sticky air was heavy and humid, and the sounds of the drills tearing into the rocky riverbed drowned out the summertime birdsong. As the sky darkened and storm clouds rolled in, the women sighed with relief in anticipation of a break in the weather. A lightning flash lit up the sky, followed by a roll of gentle thunder. Soon, they knew, the whirling drills would be silenced, as their tall, metal shafts made them far too dangerous to operate during electrical storms.

The blasting had gone on for weeks. Drill scow *John B. King* was working in the narrows off Cockburn Island in the St. Lawrence River, the longest inland seaway in the world, in an effort to make the waterway more passable. At 140 feet, the wooden boat was one of the largest of its kind in Canada. Rigged with twelve drills that were kept in working order by the onboard blacksmith shop, the boat was able to drill holes ten inches in diameter and up to thirty feet deep. The men filled the holes with dynamite, blasting the riverbed to deepen the channel and improve navigation on the busy waterway. It was hard work, but the forty-three men aboard were glad to have it. In 1930, the economy was in the grip of the Great Depression, and good jobs were scarce. Many of the men had families who relied upon them, and the scow kept food on the table for two shifts of sailors.

Mrs. McNeill and her five children were picnicking on nearby McDonald's Point when the sky turned slate gray. The youngsters had been unbothered by the clamor of the machinery on the *King*; their father was working on the scow. As the rain started to fall, Mrs. McNeill scrambled to gather their things and raced with the children to the porch of an empty summer cottage. They huddled beneath the eaves of the building, and the rain began to pound on the roof of the shelter. The family looked out at the river and watched the lightning dance across the waterway.

The US Coast Guard cutter boat *CG211* was about a half mile away from the *King* when, through the downpour, the men on deck saw a blinding flash, followed by a deafening explosion that caused the cutter to "shiver from stem to stern." Suddenly, huge waves rocked the ship as the men watched pieces of the *King* blow two hundred feet in the air, noting "the drill boat seemed to fly apart." The astonished men had just witnessed the *King* explode. When the smoke cleared, the *King* was gone, leaving only blackened wreckage bobbing in the waves. Immediately, the cutter sailed toward the disaster, the deep roar of the explosion still ringing in the ears of the crew. Three minutes later, *CG211* arrived at the field of debris where the drill scow had been and lowered her lifeboats into the water. They saw the dazed survivors, bruised and bleeding, clinging to the charred remnants of the ship, too stunned to talk. The Coast Guard crew quickly pulled the wounded sailors into the boat, ten in all, and sped to shore where ambulances were now gathering.

The women remained on the porch, shocked into silence as they watched the boat explode, throwing wreckage hundreds of feet into the air. As the smoke from the collision cleared, the women could not believe the massive boat they had watched for weeks was gone. Mrs. Walklete recalled the *King* "vanished as if by a magician's trick under smoke."

The McNeill family remembers a sudden flash of light followed by a tremendous explosion. Eight-year-old Joseph, with his eyes fixed on the river, recalled seeing "a great ball of fire and a big noise. Then the boat split in two." In a panic, his mother rushed to the water's edge, determined to save her husband, if she wasn't already too late to rescue him. Finding a rowboat close to shore, the woman struggled to move the heavy craft into the water. Rain pelted her as she wrestled with the boat until she was aided by a local man drawn to the shore by the powerful blast who helped her move the boat into the waterway. She pulled the boat's oars through the choppy water, toward the sea of scattered debris, desperately scanning the water for signs of life and finding none. She paused to catch her breath as she was approached by the *King's* tender, which was moving quickly in her direction. As the boat neared, she saw that it was manned by a family friend, Murdock Chisholm. He waved excitedly to her; inside his boat was her bruised and battered, but very much alive, husband. Found clinging to floating wreckage from the ship, he was pulled aboard the tender. Elated, Mrs. McNeill followed the tender, and the pair of boats struggled together to reach the shore. On shore and certain her husband was safe and receiving medical care, the woman collapsed, overcome by the harrowing experience. Later, rescued sailor R. A. McNeill would recall that the moment after the ship exploded, there "was a feeling that the deck had suddenly gone out from under him, then darkness until he found himself floating in the water" and grasping at boards torn loose from the ship to keep himself afloat. He continued, stating, "it was all over in an instant, and happened with such suddenness, that it was hard to tell at first what really happened. All about me were bodies of dead men and men still alive, and struggling for their lives. It was not long before I was picked up, but in the meantime, many of the bodies had disappeared beneath the waters of the St. Lawrence."

One of the men rescued by the cutter was twenty-one-year-old Leo Marion, who was in the forward, near the *King's* cookhouse, when the ship exploded. He remembers he "was thrown right up into the air, amid a geyser of sticks and rocks and broken parts of the boat." Then he was plunged underwater and pinned to the river floor by three large boulders torn free from the explosion. Twenty-eight feet beneath the surface, Marion struggled in vain to free himself from beneath the stones. With his lungs burning for air, the young sailor stopped struggling, ready to accept his fate. In that moment of stillness, he discovered he could snake his way beneath the rocks. Shimmying himself loose, he fought his way through the water, his lungs feeling as if they would burst before he broke the surface of the water. McNeill and Marion were the lucky ones; of the forty-three men aboard, by nightfall, less than half of them had been pulled from the water.

Later that evening, after it was too dark to safely continue the search for the missing in the water, the townspeople gathered at the water's edge, conducting an all-night search from the shore for the bodies of the men who had yet to be recovered. They scoured the wreckage, which scattered so widely it resembled a logjam comprised of papers, clothing, wood, and other debris. They pulled from the water Valentine's Day cards that children had made for their fathers, family photographs, and letters that had been tucked away for safekeeping, but no traces of the men had been discovered. The next morning, blurry-eyed, they filled the town's churches, each congregation holding a service for the missing sailors. Divers continued the search for days but were only able to recover thirteen of the missing men. Seventeen of the men on board that day remain forever lost.

In the days that followed, the trajectory of the tragedy became clear. Lightning struck a metal drilling pole on the boat, causing the electricity to travel through the wires of the electric detonator, igniting several tons of dynamite that was just below the boat. Those not recovered were believed to have been torn apart by the explosion.

Among those lost in the explosion were Jack Wylie and his faithful canine companion, King. The German shepherd and the sailor made news months earlier due to a near tragedy while Wylie was working to repair the ship. King was playing on the ice outside while the sailor was moving a heavy piece of machinery needed for the ship. Without warning, the ice beneath Wylie broke open, plunging the man into frigid water. Unable to swim, Jack struggled to the surface but was unable to pull himself out of the water before he lost consciousness. Seeing the

The drill scow John B. King   **Toronto Star** *Photograph Archive, Courtesy of Toronto Public Library*

sailor in distress, King leapt into the icy water and brought the unconscious man to the surface. The dog was later issued a medal of valor by the US Humane Society for his heroic rescue of Wylie. Additionally, in recognition of King's "unusual canine intelligence," he was awarded a gold medal in the Spratt's Dog Hero Awards, an honor bestowed on him just hours before his untimely death.

Today, there is a granite memorial standing on the northwest corner of Cockburn Island to commemorate the thirty men who lost their lives on June 26, 1930.

THE QUEEN OF
THE LAKES GOES
UP IN FLAMES: SS
NORONIC (1913–1949)

When the smoldering wreckage cooled enough to board the
burned-out SS *Noronic*, the search crews were stunned by the
scope of the destruction. The flames from the fire that had engulfed the
ship the night of September 17, 1949, burned so hotly it melted the
glass panes in each window and warped the vessel's steel fittings. The
boat was littered with evidence of human suffering during the chaotic
inferno. Charred skeletons clinging to each other were found throughout the vessel. Beds that had not been incinerated contained the bodies
of those overcome by smoke, then roasted alive in the flames, and the
boat was scattered with the remains of those consumed by the flames,
leaving behind only scorched skulls and blacked spines to mark their
presence. The horrors witnessed in the aftermath of the fire spurred
sweeping changes in maritime safety regulations, saving the lives of
countless future passengers, but they came too late to save the estimated
119 vacationers who perished in the deadly fire.

She was known as The Queen of the Lakes, and she had an elegance
that matched the moniker. Onboard passengers could dance the night
away in the ballroom, read a book in the library, or scan the ship's newspaper while getting a haircut in the *Noronic*'s salons. With five decks

The SS Noronic *on her maiden voyage* **WikiCommons**

and the ability to carry eight hundred people, the six-thousand-ton ship was the largest passenger ship in service on the Great Lakes. She set sail on September 14, 1949, for a seven-day pleasure cruise around the Lakes.

Captain William Taylor led the ship as she carried 524 passengers and 171 crew when she docked at Pier Nine in the Toronto Harbour at seven in the evening on September 16. Many of the passengers and all but approximately seventeen of the crew left the ship to explore Ontario's capital city. Those who remained on board enjoyed a meal in the dining room or went to the lounge to dance and sip cocktails. While most passengers began making their way to their cabins at some time after ten that night, a few merrymakers continued the fun until well after midnight. Don Church, a fire insurance specialist, was among those late-night revelers.

Returning to his cabin at half past two in the morning, Church noticed a haze in the air and the familiar smell of burning. Following the scent, the haze grew into smoke, and the man discovered a fire in a locked linen closet on the port side of the ship, near the staterooms. Church alerted a bellboy of the blaze behind the locked door. Neither man pulled the fire alarm; instead, the bellboy ran to get the keys needed to open the closet. Returning quickly, the bellboy unlocked the door, and when he opened the linen closet door, the fire exploded into the hallway, igniting the lemon-oil-polished wood paneling that lined the walls. Church and two members of the ship's crew attacked the flames with fire extinguishers, to no avail. The men then grabbed the ship's firehose. Church aimed the hose at the blaze, but no water came out. Frustrated, he dropped the useless hose and ran to alert his family of the danger.

Thirty minutes after the fire was discovered, and with half of the ship's decks now ablaze, the first mate sounded the fire alarm, but it too failed to do its job. The whistle alert to notify passengers and crew of a fire on board a ship is three short blasts, followed by a long blast. The *Noronic*'s whistle malfunctioned during the critical attempt to sound the warning, giving out only a single long blast. The endless shrill howl from the whistle made it impossible to hear safety announcements, or anything else, above the high-pitched din.

The few crewmembers that were on duty at that hour had not been trained to handle this type of crisis. With the captain still in the city, the crew fled while sleeping passengers were trapped in their rooms by the ever-growing flames. As passengers awoke to realize the ship was on fire, the chaos of the night began. In the panicked exodus from the blaze, some passengers were trampled in the hallways. Others, unable to navigate the smoke- and flame-filled passageways, instead smashed through the windows of their rooms, moving through the shattered panes of glass toward freedom. Some frantically ran along the upper decks, not knowing how to get off the engulfed ship, often slipping on walkways now slick with blood.

Stairwells acted as chimneys, funneling oxygen to feed the hungry flames, and the fire continued to grow. Screams of terror joined the shriek of the boat's whistle as passengers scrambled down ropes and cables in an attempt to save their lives. One reporter on the scene recalled watching passengers escape from the ship, noting "some had their clothing ablaze and were screaming with pain. Others were cut, their faces masks of blood." For those trapped on the decks, the only way to escape was jumping off the side of the ship nearest to the pier.

The Noronic *engulfed in flames on that fateful September morning in 1949* **WikiCommons/ City of Toronto Archives**

It was difficult to accurately aim for the thin strip of water between the boat and the concrete pier; this dangerous means of exit was fatal for some. Bodies hit the pier, and a few, after failing to clear the ship when they jumped, hit the decks below. Soon, corpses dotted the water around the boat. A ladder was raised to the ship to aid in the evacuation, but in the clamor to escape, more people climbed onto the ladder than the lifeline could support, and it snapped, plunging the panicked passengers into the water.

Early responders to the crisis, constables Ronald Anderson and Warren Shaddock, jumped into the water to rescue the injured. By the time the firefighters arrived, the top three decks of the ship were fully aflame. Many of the police and firefighters on the scene were World War II combat veterans whose wartime experience allowed them to better deal with the nightmare unfolding before them. One firefighter recalled the flames "swept from the bow to stern and from waterline to mast, which roared through it with lightning speed." Flames jutted from the ship's portholes. The hull burned white-hot, causing the decks to buckle. Millions of gallons of water were directed at the blaze, yet it continued to rage. Firefighters were forced to evacuate the area when the ship began to list in response to the deluge of water, returning after the ship righted itself.

The flames lit up the night sky, drawing Toronto residents from miles around to the lakefront to watch the tragedy develop. Police held back crowds as thousands flocked to the area. Police cruisers and taxicabs worked with the ambulances to ferry the injured to area hospitals. Before dawn, the cars were splattered with blood, and a heavy smell of smoke permeated the interiors. Chaplains administered last rites to the critically injured throughout the night. When it appeared things could get no worse, "there were several small explosions on the front of the upper deck. Within moments, the entire front upper deck collapsed with a roar." The pieces of the burning ship fell into the dark waters of Lake Ontario with a hiss.

As the sun rose, the early morning light showed the ship was "fully gutted from mast to waterline." A Canadian journalist, Edwin Feeny, recalled the scene as "a horrible picture of charred remains amid foot deep embers and melted glass." As rescuers waded through the wreckage, they came upon victims who "were not more than ash and a pile of jewelry." Firefighters removing the charred remains of the dead from the ship eventually ran out of tarps to cover the corpses. Visibly shaken men began stacking the bodies on the pier until midmorning, when it became clear there were too many dead to be handled on the scene. Quickly, a makeshift mortuary was created in the nearby Canadian National Exposition Center's Horticulture Building. The bodies below the ship's waterline remained in the burned-out skeleton of the boat for days, until the "tens of thousands of gallons of water" inside the ship could be pumped out so the bodies could be retrieved.

The tragedy ushered in a new era of safety regulations for passenger boats on the Great Lakes. The expense involved in retrofitting the cruisers with the required safety features effectively ended pleasure cruising on the Lakes. While critical in the evolution of maritime regulations, the lasting impact of the *Noronic* fire reveals itself in an unusual way in the Toronto Harbour. Many believe the terrible events of that fall evening in 1949 caused the area to be haunted by the spirits of passengers who lost their lives in the fire. The supernatural activity appears to be focused in the area of Pier Nine and the former Canadian National Exposition Center's Horticulture building. While the building has changed hands and functions many times since it was used as a makeshift morgue, it appears the spirits of those lost in the tragic fire still linger within its walls. Today, the former horticulture center is a stop on a number of Toronto ghost tours, and eerie occurrences in the building are not uncommon.

There have been countless speculations, but what caused the fire in the linen closet that began the tragedy has never been determined; however outdated onboard safety measures and a lack of leadership on behalf of the captain and the boat's owners were cited as the cause for the tragedy's high death toll. During the proceedings following the fire, it was often noted that not a single member of the crew was among the 119 victims who perished that night. Today, only a handful of relics from the destroyed ship, markers honoring the dead, and the restless spirits of those who lost their lives on that fatal voyage are all that remains of the one-time Queen of the Lakes.

LAKE SUPERIOR

Lake Superior is the largest of the Great Lakes, with a circumference of 31,700 square miles. The average depth of the lake is 438 feet, measuring 1,333 feet at its deepest point, representing 10 percent of all of the Earth's fresh surface water. The highest wave recorded on the lake measured thirty-one feet, and winds over 60 miles an hour are not uncommon. The lake's extreme weather, which includes blizzards with snowfall measured in feet, rather than inches, and windchills exceeding minus-50 degrees Fahrenheit, is the result of cold arctic air from Canada mixing with warm air from the Gulf of Mexico. This dangerous weather pattern, coupled with the lake's hidden shoals, makes it a hazardous body of water to sail.

There is no definitive answer to the number of shipwrecks that have occurred on Lake Superior; however, the Great Lakes Shipwreck Museum in Whitefish Point, Michigan, indicates there are 550 known wrecks in the lake. Some sources estimate that ten thousand people have lost their lives in Superior, many of those bodies having never been recovered. The icy lake, whose average temperature is just 36 degrees Fahrenheit, is well known for not "giving up her dead." The inability to recover bodies from the lake is due to its low temperatures. Often bodies resurface because the bacteria that feed on the flesh of the corpses creates gas, which makes the bodies buoyant. Superior's water is too cold for the bacteria to thrive, keeping many bodies far beneath the waves.

The lake is popularly known as "Gitche Gumee," a name which Henry Wadsworth Longfellow used in his 1855 *The Song of Hiawatha*.

The classic piece of American literature tells the story of a love affair between an indigenous couple set on the shore of Lake Superior. Longfellow borrowed the term from the Ojibwe language, believing it meant "Big Sea Water." The first published dictionary of the Ojibwe language, released in 1878, indicated the term for Lake Superior was *Otchipwe-kitchi-gami*, which means "the sea of the Ojibwe people." Still used as a synonym for the lake, today it is more common to see the name spelled *gichi-gami* or *gitchi-gami*, which is closer to the original Ojibwe term Longfellow meant to use.

Isle Royale

Surrounded by a chain of 450 smaller islands, the isle itself is forty-five miles long and nine miles wide. It is the largest island in Lake Superior and part of what is known as the Superior Shoal, an area marked by rocky, hidden reefs created by volcanic eruptions that occurred before the Great Lakes were formed. This area is among the most treacherous on the lake and is the location of many shipwrecks. The remote area, once known as the Voyagers Highway, was traveled by canoe by indigenous people and later by white settlers involved in fur trapping and trade. The discovery of silver and copper created a mining industry in the area and brought increased traffic and larger boats to the reef-filled area. Now a national park, the island has no permanent residents and does not allow automobiles. Despite being identified as the least visited of all of the national parks, the wilderness hideaway still draws an estimated eighteen thousand tourists a year.

Lighthouses

The island has four lighthouses warning sailors of the dangers that lurk below Superior's cold waters. The Rock Harbor lighthouse is the oldest in Isle Royale and was built in 1855. The fifty-foot tower marks the harbor's westernmost entrance. Now being operated as a museum in the Isle Royale National Park, the lighthouse ceased operation at the close of the 1879 shipping season. In 1875 a second lighthouse, the Isle Royale, was constructed on Menagerie Island. Located at the mouth of the Siskiwit Bay, the sixty-one-foot tower was erected near a busy copper mine. Still in use, this now automated lighthouse uses solar power to send out its beacon. The third lighthouse built, the Passage Island lighthouse, is considered to be the most important of the quartet, as it marks the dangerous waterway between Blake Point and Passage Island. Sailors navigating the area have likened it to "thread(ing) the needle," as the narrow passage is only three and a quarter miles wide. When Passage Island opened in 1882, it was originally outfitted with a fog bell, which was soon replaced with a fog whistle and joined the forty-four-foot light tower. Lastly, the Rock of Ages lighthouse was erected in 1908. Towering over the other lighthouses at 117 feet high, it was automated in 1978. On a clear night, its light can be seen for twenty-nine miles, making her one of the most powerful beacons on the Great Lakes.

Shipwrecks

The Isle Royale, with its severe weather patterns and rocky reefs, is a perilous area that has had twenty-five major wrecks, with ten of them listed on the National Register of Historic Places. Remaining under the waves, these sunken ships are time capsules of maritime history. The following ships bring in thousands of divers each year to explore the world beneath the surface of the water.

Algoma (1883–1885)

The screw steamer ran aground on the southeast shore of Mott Island. The ship was torn in half by the powerful waves. The heavy seas dashed the bodies of those attempting to flee the ship against the rocks, pulverizing them. Of the sixty people on board the ship, only fourteen survived, making it one of Lake Superior's most deadly wrecks.

America (1898–1928)

The helm of the steel freighter was handed over to an inexperienced first mate as the ship was leaving Washington Harbor. Within five minutes of departure, the ship hit a hidden reef. All forty-seven people aboard were evacuated on lifeboats and survived.

Chester A. Congdon (1907–1918)

Named for the Minnesota lawyer who made his fortune in mining and then entered state politics, the steel freighter ran aground in heavy fog. Beneath the waves in a place now called Congdon Shoal, this wreck without fatalities was notable for being the first wreck on Lake Superior to be valued at over one million dollars.

Cumberland (1871–1877)

The wooden-hulled passenger steamer struck a reef near the Rock of Ages lighthouse. No fatalities were involved in this accident.

Emperor (1910–1947)

The steel freighter struck Canoe Rocks due to a navigation error and began taking on water quickly. Within thirty minutes the 525-foot, 10,000-ton ship sank. It went down so quickly that the portside lifeboat was pulled under by the powerful suction created by the sinking wreck. Twelve men died, including the captain and first mate, and fifteen crew were rescued by the US Coast Guard.

George M. Cox (1901–1933)

Formerly known as the USS *Puritan*, this steel passenger screw steamer was decommissioned in 1919. She struck the Rock of Ages reef on her maiden voyage under her new name. All aboard survived the wreck.

Glenlyon (1893–1924)

The package freighter struck the reef off Menagerie Island while seeking safe harbor during a heavy storm. The ship's pumps kept the sailors above water until they could be rescued, and there were no fatalities.

Henry Chisholm (1880–1898)

The wooden steamer, named for the Ohioan who made his fortune in the steel industry, wrecked when she hit the Rock of Ages reef while traveling at full speed. All sixteen aboard survived the accident.

Kamloops (1924–1927)

The package freighter disappeared with all of her crew during a brutal winter storm. She was lost until 1977 when she was found by divers.

Monarch (1890–1906)

The ship hit the rocks on the coldest day of 1906. With just one fatality, the remaining people on board managed to survive for several days until they could be reached by rescuers.

View from Lookout Louise, Isle Royale National Park, Rock Harbor, Michigan **Creative Commons Corvair Owner is licensed under CC BY-SA 2.0**

Superior's Shipwreck Coast

Another notoriously dangerous stretch of water on the lake is the area known as "Shipwreck Coast," or sometimes more colorfully as "Graveyard Coast." Not all who study the area agree on the span of this legendary area along the northern coast of Michigan's upper peninsula, but many agree that Whitefish Point is in the heart of the region where an estimated two hundred ships fell below the surface of the water. Nearby beautiful Pictured Rocks, with its stunning sandstone cliffs, has been the site of an estimated fifty wrecks. Great Lakes historian Frederick Stonehouse, who has written extensively about the area, quoted the 1871 *Marquette Mining Journal*, which stated, "in all navigation of Lake Superior, there is none more dreaded by the mariner than that from Whitefish Point to Grand Island." His research indicates that white settlers documented the danger of the area as far back as 1622. The rocky hidden reefs, rough waters, heavy fog, and even smoke from onshore forest fires have all worked together to make this area among the deadliest on the lake.

Like Isle Royale, the traffic dramatically increased in the area with the development in the mining industry, and this traffic brought the need for lighthouses. Along the one-hundred-mile stretch between Grand Island and Whitefish Point, nine lighthouses were erected in an effort to keep the expensive ships and their valuable cargo safe from the hazardous shoals. The first of the ennead was the lighthouse at Whitefish Point, which was lit in 1849. The lighthouse is now part of the Great Lakes Shipwreck Museum. The largest of the group is the Au Sable Point Light Station, which warns sailors of the shallow sandstone shoals, with some of the rock formations jutting up to just six feet beneath the surface of the water. At eighty-seven feet tall, the still-active station was automated in 1958.

The area is a mecca for freshwater divers eager to explore shipwrecks. The clear water allows for shallow wrecks to be viewed from aboard glass-bottomed ships, and wreckage from ships sunk long ago still washes up on local beaches. Among the best-known ships to have succumbed to the rocky reefs and powerful seas of the Shipwreck Coast are the following:

Bermuda (1860–1870)
Also known as the Murray Bay wreck, it lies in waters so shallow it can be explored by snorkelers.

Comet (1857–1875)

The ship was rammed by the passing *Manitoba*, breaking the *Comet* in two. She sank within five minutes and took the lives of eleven of the twenty-one men on board. She is considered one of the true "treasure ships" in Superior because she sunk carrying a notable amount of silver ore.

Edmund Fitzgerald (1958–1975)

The steel freighter went down in heavy seas and gale-force winds. The modern-era disaster is Superior's best-known wreck.

Elma (1873–1895)

The schooner was lost during a storm and is sunk in shallow waters by Pictured Rocks. Of the nine aboard, there was only one fatality.

HE Runnels (1893–1919)

Run aground while looking for safe harbor from driving snow and gale-force winds near Grand Marais. All seventeen crewmen were saved in an effort so daring the rescuers were awarded medals for their bravery.

John B. Cowle (1902–1909)

Named for Cleveland shipbuilder John Beswick Cowle, the ship was obscured by heavy fog when she was wrecked in a collision. The ship sank in three minutes, and only ten of the twenty-four crewmen survived.

Manhattan (1887–1903)

Another popular wreck with divers, this wooden ship was stranded and burned after striking Grand Island.

Nelson (1866–1899)

The three-mast schooner was rediscovered in 2014. She met heavy winds and ice. The captain evacuated the nine others aboard into the lifeboat, then discovered too late the lifeboat was still attached to the rapidly sinking ship. All aboard the lifeboat perished, making the captain the only survivor of the ten people aboard.

Smith Moore (1880–1889)

Among Pictured Rocks National Lakeshore's most popular attractions, the *Smith Moore* is a favorite with freshwater divers. Sunk as the result of a collision, this wreck had no fatalities.

Superior City (1898–1920)

The steel freighter was rammed by the passing *Willis L. King*, causing a breach in the ship. The cold water that rushed into the *Superior City* caused its boiler to explode. Only four of the thirty-three crew and passengers aboard escaped alive.

A FATE FORETOLD:
SS *WESTERN RESERVE*
(1890–1892)

S he was big, she was fast, and she was one of the first steel ships to sail on the Great Lakes. This sleek, modern workhorse was thought to be indestructible. The 2,400-ton behemoth was just a shade longer than a football field at 301 feet in length. Designed to haul ore and other heavy loads, she set speed and cargo-load records on the Lakes during her brief career. Owned by the newly minted millionaire businessman Peter G. Minch, a master seaman and captain who grew up sailing the Lakes with his father, the ship was led by the experienced Captain Albert Myers. The fine boat and her capable crew were the envy of many on the Lakes.

In late summer, the Ohio businessman with a love of being on the water decided to turn a run on the finest ship in his fleet into a pleasure cruise for his family. His wife, Anna, prepared their children, ten-year-old Charlie and six-year-old Florence, for the outing and invited her sister and nine-year-old niece, Bertha, to accompany them on their jaunt through the Lakes. The vacationers were joined by a crew of twenty-one. The *Western Reserve* set sail from Cleveland on August 28, 1892, bound for Two Harbors, Minnesota, and a load of iron ore. Empty when she left, the ship swiftly moved through Lakes Erie and Huron toward her destination in Lake Superior.

By August 30, the *Western Reserve* was in Lake Superior. The fine weather that marked the early leg of their journey faded, and the ship found itself in the midst of a rare August gale. The ship was battered by heavy northwest winds. Minch urged Myers to move beyond the protection provided by Point Iroquois and press on into the lake, confident the sturdy ship could handle the heavy winds and waves. The empty ship, riding high in the waves, was being punished by the storm. Finally, the ship could take no more, and at nine in the evening, everyone aboard heard a tremendous crashing sound. It was soon discovered the steel ship had cracked through her deck, just forward of her boiler room, and was splitting in two. The gap between the two sides of the ship widened rapidly as water rushed in and the waves pulled the boat apart. As the steel trusses snapped and the mainmast began to fall, the crew lowered the lifeboats into the turbulent waves.

A metal and a wooden yawl were in the water, waiting to be filled with passengers and crew. Despite the rapidly sinking ship, everyone calmly boarded the boats. Minch and his family, and some of the crew, boarded the wooden boat, and the remaining crew filled the metal ship. With its engines still running, the massive freighter disappeared beneath the waves in less than ten minutes. Before the last traces of the mighty ship fell to the bottom of the lake, the metal yawl capsized in the heavy waves. The wooden yawl rushed toward the capsized boat to come to the aid of the crewmembers plunged into the lake. The passengers scanned the waves anxiously, but only two crewmen fought their way back to the surface: Carl Myers, son of the ship's captain, and Harry Stewart, a wheelman. The two survivors were pulled aboard the wooden yawl, and the group began their sixty-mile journey to the shore.

Now dangerously overweight, the wooden yawl was just one foot above the waterline. The heavy waves of the August gale relentlessly filled the low-riding boat, forcing the passengers to bail out the boat without ceasing, using the one bucket aboard and the few hats that remained on the heads of the men when they escaped the sinking freighter to remove the lake water that pooled at the bottom of the boat. Cold, wet, and under constant siege from the lake, the group battled through the night to stay alive. Hope was ignited when the weather-battered yawl saw the red light of a nearby freighter. Without a lamp, the wooden boat could not signal the freighter for help, so they screamed as loud as they could and gestured with as much animation as their precarious position allowed. When it was clear the freighter did not notice them, they made a frantic attempt to attract attention by setting a match to the shawl resting on the shoulders of one of the sisters. The shawl, like everything else in the boat, was too wet to ignite. Despite their best efforts, they could not make themselves seen or heard through the gale that continued to rage. Defeated after half an hour of hopeful noise, the group resumed their efforts to keep their embattled boat afloat.

They bailed the wooden yawl through the night, and by seven the next morning, the group spotted land on the horizon. The cold, exhausted group felt their hopes rise again as the shore grew ever nearer. The sisters, both wearing life jackets, clung tightly to their children as the waves pushed the boat toward land. Within a mile of the shore, the yawl was caught in a massive wave, capsizing the boat. For a few moments, the air was filled with the frightened screams of women and the moan of pain from a man, and then, all was silent. Crewman Harry Stewart looked around him, and he discovered his was the only head above the waves. He clung to the life preserver he grabbed as he was dumped out of the boat and realized he was the only one from the *Western Reserve* who was still alive. Drained from his night on the yawl, Stewart had little energy left to swim to shore, but he was determined to reach the beach. Relying on the life preserver, and drifting in and out of consciousness, it took the twenty-four-year-old man two hours to travel the mile to shore.

Once Stewart reached the beach, he had little opportunity to celebrate. He calculated he was ten miles away from Deer Park Life-Saving Station, and he knew reaching the station was his only hope for survival. After laying on the beach for nearly an hour, the sailor summoned his strength and began the long walk toward salvation. He stumbled through the woods, sometimes crawling when he grew too weak to walk. Stewart fought the obstacles and reached the doorstep of the Deer Park Station.

The bloodied and battered sailor told the story of the ordeal to the Deer Park employee, Benjamin Tru(e)dell. Stewart watched the man's face grow pale as he recounted the sinking of the indestructible *Western Reserve*. Trudell turned to his colleagues to see their shocked faces. The night before, Trudell slept fitfully and awoke with a jolt after dreaming of a ship sinking on Lake Superior. So vivid was the dream that the man could not shake the feeling of dread, so he dressed and made a visit to the nighttime watchman. He recounted his disturbing dream and described the ship sinking in a storm and the survivors drowning in heavy waves. He continued, telling of walking the beach to look for survivors of the wreck when he encountered a well-dressed man who rose from the surf, shook Trudell's hand, and then silently pointed to the lake. The watchmen laughed at the dream and assured Trudell that there had been no notice of a ship in trouble, then told him to go back to bed. Shaken and unable to free himself from the sense of dread the dream brought him, he returned to his bed. Hearing Stewart tell the story of the *Western Reserve*'s fate, Trudell and his colleagues could not help but note the eerie similarities between the sinking of the steel freighter and his disturbing dream.

The crew of the Deer Park Station rushed down to the beach in search of survivors of the wreck. The men recovered the wooden yawl, but it was empty. As they continued along the beach, they discovered the bodies of a man and a woman. The man, lying face down in the sand, was no stranger to Trudell; he instantly recognized the body as the smartly dressed man from his dream the night before. As the men removed the body from the sand, the drowned man's engraved wristwatch confirmed his identity; it was Peter Minch. Some who convey this strange tale claim that it was Trudell who turned the body over to reveal its face, and when he did, the lifeless hand of the corpse fell into Trudell's hand, mimicking the handshake Trudell had dreamed of the night before. In the days following, the men continued to comb the beach, and eventually they recovered sixteen bodies from the ship, including four of the six members of the Minch family. The men buried the waterlogged bodies on a wood bluff above the beach, where they washed ashore, saying a simple prayer over the shallow grave. The bodies of the Minch family, and a few of the other corpses, were claimed by their families, exhumed, and sent to cemeteries for permanent interment.

Questions remained about how the mighty *Western Reserve* could have broken in two. There were many theories ranging from poor construction to careless sailing, but the probable answer was determined months later when the *Western Reserve*'s sister ship, the *W. H. Gilcher,* sunk on Lake Michigan, taking all men aboard with her. After an investigation, it was determined both ships were built with brittle steel. Steel containing sulfur, phosphorus, and other contaminants becomes brittle in cold water, making it dangerous for the frigid waterways of the Great Lakes. Many believe brittle steel was a contributing factor to the sinking of the famous *Titanic*.

In the years that followed, many attempts were made to find the *Western Reserve*, but she remains lost beneath the waves. Thought to lie between four hundred and six hundred feet beneath the surface of the lake, she may never be recovered. Sole survivor Harry Stewart continued to earn his living as a sailor and eventually earned the rank of captain. He died in 1938 at age seventy. Despite never sailing on the *Western Reserve*, Benjamin Trudell became forever linked to the sinking of the freighter due to his strange dream that seemed to predict the disaster. Trudell continued to sail until he retired from the US Coast Guard in 1923. He died in 1954 at age eighty-two. He, and his often-retold tale, are an inextricable part of Lake Superior lore.

Today, few mention the *Western Reserve* without stating that she has become a member of the fleet of ghost ships still rumored to sail the treacherous waters of Lake Superior. Some who sail near the Deer Park Station swear that, on a calm night, the sounds of laughter and the murmur of distant conversation can be heard when this ghostly ship sails through the fog before gently gliding out of sight.

LAKE SUPERIOR'S *FLYING DUTCHMAN*: SS *BANNOCKBURN* (1893–1902)

The Legend of the *Flying Dutchman* is a centuries-old tale that recounts the tortured existence of a captain cursed to forever sail the seas. The tale warns that any boat that encounters the ship and her ghostly crew will soon encounter misfortune. The SS *Bannockburn* has earned the moniker of the *Flying Dutchman* of Lake Superior because this ship, easily identified by her unique silhouette and three masts, continues to be spotted sailing the lake, despite disappearing beneath her unforgiving waves in 1902.

The 245-foot-long steel freighter set sail from Port Arthur with 85,000 bushels of wheat on the morning of November 21, 1902. Captain George R. Wood, the oldest man on the ship at age thirty-seven, was charged with leading twenty-one young sailors, most between the ages of seventeen and twenty, with the youngest crewman being a sixteen-year-old wheelman who was the sole supporter of his four orphaned siblings. The skies were clear and the sailing was easy when the ship left port, but by midday the *Bannockburn* found herself in a whistling gale. Captain James McMaugh of the *Algonquin* spotted the easily identifiable *Bannockburn* through the fog and haze and recorded the sighting in his log. She was plowing through choppy waters while

The Bannockburn *in dry dock* **WikiCommons Maritime History of the Great Lakes, the Barb Carson Collection**

bucking a headwind but was holding her own against the harsh weather. Minutes later, when he glanced up from his writing desk, McMaugh noticed the ship vanished from view. Puzzled, but not concerned, McMaugh thought the ship had been obscured by heavy fog.

As the day turned to night, the gale winds grew in intensity, and Superior's high waves pummeled boats on the water. It was remembered by crewmember Fred Landon of the *Huronic* as the worst storm of the season. While recording the events of the day in his diary, Landon noted that around eleven that night, he saw the *Bannockburn* sailing through the storm without a struggle. This uneventful sighting may have been the last glimpse anyone had of the sturdy steel freighter.

When the boat did not reach its destination, it was assumed she found a safe harbor to shelter herself from the storm. Once the weather cleared and the ship did not appear in port, fears about the fate of the *Bannockburn* began to spread. There were a number of reports that the ship had run aground on some of the lake's northern islands, giving the families of the crewmen hope that the sailors would be found safe, but each sighting proved to be false. After days of searching, the ship was declared lost on November 30, 1902. The whereabouts of the SS *Bannockburn* remain unknown to this day. Not a single member of the crew was ever recovered, and the only evidence of the ship that has ever been found was a single lifeboat oar with the ship's name etched upon it, which washed up many months after the freighter mysteriously disappeared.

Despite being declared lost in 1902, the SS *Bannockburn* and her distinct silhouette are still spotted on Lake Superior to this day. There are generations of sailors who have claimed to see the three-mast ship emerge from the fog and sail by, her pilothouse dark and her running lights glowing through the haze. These sightings are most common during the dangerous month of November and often occur in conjunction with an incoming storm or other peril on the waterway. The most famous of these ghostly sightings was made by the crew of the freighter *Walter A. Hitchinson*, shortly after the close of World War II.

The *Hitchinson* was caught in a storm and had iced up so badly that she had lost her electronics and navigation tools. To prevent capsizing in the heavy waves, she sailed close to shore, but without the aid of her sensors, the crew could not tell how close they were to dangerous jagged rocks near the shore, which hid just beneath the surface of the relentless storm waves. As the crew continued to creep along the shoreline, they suddenly spotted the *Bannockburn* approximately one hundred yards away, sailing straight toward the struggling *Hitchinson*. Shocked by the ship's sudden appearance, the captain ordered the crew to sharply veer to the portside to avoid the oncoming ship. While battling the heavy waves, the crewmen claimed to have watched the *Bannockburn* pass astern of the *Hitchinson*, and then run aground on a hidden cluster of rocks. Before their eyes, they saw the steel freighter ripped open by the obstacle, and then quickly vanish from their sight. Dumbfounded by what they had just seen, it took the crew very little time to realize that had the *Bannockburn* not sailed toward them and forced them to change course, it would be their ship which would have been torn apart by the jagged stones.

Today, sightings of the ship that mysteriously disappeared in 1902 continue. Some of these tales include otherworldly details, like accounts of a crew of skeletons manning the massive ship, that might make the legends surrounding the SS *Bannockburn* easy for the skeptical to dismiss. What remains true is that more than one hundred years after she set sail, those who earn their living on Lake Superior's water still scan the horizon for the three-mast ship and heed her warnings if they catch a glimpse of her emerging from the fog with her running lights aglow.

THE LONG WEEKEND: SS *MONARCH* (1890–1906)

John D. McCallum accepted his award with pride. The Royal Canadian Humane Society issued him a Bronze Medal for Bravery in honor of his heroic actions during the sinking of the SS *Monarch*. Exactly how he did it remains debated, but somehow John D. McCallum managed to run a line from the failing ship to the ice-coated, rocky shore of Isle Royale. Some say he jumped, while others say he swung on the rope like a pendulum then launched himself ashore. However he did it, the stout-hearted man battled gale-force winds and a blinding snowstorm while armed with nothing more than a rope and wooden ladder to create a lifeline that allowed all but one person aboard to flee the wreck.

McCallum might have won an award, but he was far from the only person whose courage and ingenuity were on display during the bitter-cold December days in 1906 when the passengers and crew of the *Monarch* were marooned on an uninhabited rocky shoal. Fighting hunger, snow, and the unrelenting frigid wind, the group worked together to stay alive.

It was the final run of the year. The vessel left Port Arthur after sunset on December 9, 1933. The SS *Monarch*, loaded with freight and just a handful of passengers, fought through the gale-force winds as they sailed into the night. The winds and seas were heavy as they sailed through the blizzard. The snow, falling quickly, reduced visibility to less than fifty feet, and Captain Teddy Robertson had just discovered his compass was no longer working. They were nine hundred yards west of Blake Point, on the northeast tip of Isle Royale, when the *Monarch*'s luck ran out. At half-past nine that evening, the ship ran into the solid rock wall known as the Palisades.

The collision reverberated through the boat, and the captain ordered the engineers to take the 240-foot ship to "full astern." Engineer Samuel Beatty disobeyed the command and held the ship against the rocks as he knew the collision had torn a hole into the bow of the ship. His quick thinking saved the lives of those aboard the ship that was rapidly filling with water. Soon, lifeboats were lowered, and McCallum strung a lifeline to the icy shoal.

When the group made it to shore, they were not yet safe. The island had no shelter and no way for them to communicate their need for help. Cold and wet, they gathered wood to create a fire on the unsettled island. Once the fire was lit, their chances of surviving the night greatly increased. Their waterlogged clothes were frozen solid by the ceaseless winds, and they huddled around the flames to stay warm as the snow continued to fly. A few men trudged through the snow and tore bare branches from the trees to create a crude windbreak to protect the group from the storm. Only one blanket made it onto the island, and they gave it to the only woman on board, kitchen worker Rachel McCormick. With the storm still raging around them, they fed the fire throughout the night and waited for the sun to rise.

On Friday morning, a few men climbed to higher ground to light a second fire, in hopes of attracting a passing boat or a nearby lighthouse. No one knew they were stranded on the island, and they had no means of sending out a call for help. In need of supplies, a few of the men braved the rough waters and made it back to the partially submerged *Monarch*. Hunger motivated the men to reboard the wrecked ship. In need of food, one crewmember tied a rope to his waist and was lowered into the galley to gather what he could salvage from the kitchen. A slab of damaged bacon and a few baked goods were all that could be retrieved from the boat, and they were joined by a case of canned salmon and a bag of flour that had washed to shore. The men gathered the fallen ship's sails, using them to create a shelter for the group.

Without a pan to cook in, McCormick cooked the flapjacks she made with the flour that washed ashore in the ashes of the fire. Sooty and solid, the survivors would later remember that they "resembled a piece of frozen asphalt block," but they were enough to keep the group going. As the sun set Friday evening, the storm had not yet abated. They continued to keep both fires burning on the island as they began their second night as castaways.

On Saturday morning, the group lit a third fire on the island, desperate for someone on the lake to notice the stranded group. The nearby Passage Island Lighthouse keeper could see the fires burning on Blake Point, but the heavy waves made it impossible for him to reach the *Monarch* survivors in the lighthouse's small, wooden boat. Unable to offer aid, all he could do was keep an eye on the island and hope the passengers and crew could stay alive long enough to be rescued.

Eventually, the storm quieted just enough for the lightkeeper to row the four miles between Passage Island and Blake Point. The waves were still too heavy for him to navigate the rocky shoals, and he was not able to reach land. Steeling himself against the icy waters, purser Reginald Beaumont swam out of the small boat and returned to the lighthouse with the keeper where the pair busied signaling area boats that help was needed. The nearby *Edmonton* responded to their signal and sailed to the Isle Royale to render aid but realized they could not get close enough to the jagged reef to reach the *Monarch* survivors. Beginning their third night on the island, the castaways watched the *Edmonton* sail away toward Port Arthur.

The *Edmonton* reached Port Arthur at two in the morning bearing the news of the wrecked *Monarch* and its stranded passengers and crew. Quickly a rescue party was organized, and by six Sunday morning, rescue boats had set sail to Blake Point. The survivors' excitement of seeing the rescue boats on the horizon was tempered when they realized their ordeal was not yet over. The boats were still unable to travel through the rocky shoals as the waves were still heavy. To get off the island, the cold, hungry, and exhausted survivors would have to hike across the island to a port that was safer for the boats. Despite spending three stormy nights on the island without shelter and scant food, each of the castaways that made it to the island left alive and without permanent injury.

Once safely back in Port Arthur, the losses of the journey could finally be tallied. The *Monarch* broke into pieces in the rough waters and then sunk to the bottom of the lake in the days following the collision. Both the ship and the cargo were declared total losses, and the wreck was noted as the largest financial loss of the shipping season on the Great Lakes. Forty-one people were taken alive from the island and had frostbite severe enough to warrant amputations, which was an outcome worth celebrating, but not everyone walked away from the wreck. Eighteen-year-old watchman Jacques was lost in the icy waves as he tried to flee the failing ship. He had only worked on the lake for a few months before being pulled into his watery grave. Today, the *Monarch* is one of the ten notable wrecks divers explore in the shoals off Isle Royale. The cold water and the protected status of the region preserve a bounty of maritime history that lies below the surface of the water.

THE STEEP PRICE OF CUTTING COSTS: *GUNILDA* (1897–1911)

William Harkness was among the richest men in the United States in 1911. The son of Stephen Harkness, one of the initial investors in Rockefeller's Standard Oil Company, he was used to the best of everything money could buy. Ohio born and Yale educated, Harkness was an avid yachtsman who belonged to both the New York Yacht Club and the Seawanhaka Corinthian Yacht Club. The tycoon owned a number of boats, but none was finer than the *Gunilda*, a 195-foot steel steam yacht. The one-time flagship of the New York Yacht Club, the boat had every luxury that could be offered a well-heeled traveler of the gilded age. Notably fast, she was outfitted with gleaming brass and rich mahogany throughout the ship and accented with gold leafing for a touch of opulence that was reflective of Harkness's great wealth.

On July 19, 1911, *Gunilda* set sail with Captain Alexander Corkum at the helm, aided by a crew of twenty. Harkness and his guests, Mrs. and Mr. J. H. Harding of New York, were on board and anticipating fishing in the northern Lake Superior town of Rossport. Along the way, the boat would stop at Harkness' Georgian Bay summer home where his family was vacationing so his wife and two children, Louise, age nine, and Billy, age five, could board the ship and join the trip.

The trip was a pleasant one that stretched out over many weeks, and the group finally reached the Nipigon Bay on August 11. The area was as well known for its excellent fishing as it was for its treacherous topography. Navigating through the cluster of islands and shoals to reach Rossport was a difficult task, which was made more challenging by notoriously inaccurate maritime maps of the area. It was recommended that the large ship should hire a local guide to navigate through the dangerous waterway studded with jagged rocks. Harkness balked at the $15 charge for a local guide, certain he was being gouged by crafty locals who wanted to make a quick profit off the millionaire. Thinking the waterway was nothing that could not be handled by the experienced Captain Corkum, Harkness ordered that ship to continue sailing through the dangerous waterway towards Rossport.

The *Gunilda* had not passed Copper Island before she was caught in the McGarvey Shoal. Lurking three feet below the waterline, the ship struck what appeared to be a rock but was actually a sheer cliff of rock soaring up from a depth of 280 feet. Unseen in the dense fog, the yacht struck the rock with such force it jolted the passengers out of their sleeping berths. While little harm had come to the passengers or the ship, the *Gunilda* was thrust out of the water and would need to be towed off the rock.

When the tugboat captain arrived to get the yacht back into the water, he determined that a second boat would be needed to safely free the ship. The incredulous Harkness had learned no lessons from his refusal to hire a local guide. Again, thinking he was being hoodwinked by a greedy local, he rejected the man's assessment that a second tow was needed, and reluctantly, the tugboat began to pull the *Gunilda* off the rock that had trapped her. So confident was Harkness that that tow would be successful, none of the boat's windows or hatches had been secured before work began.

True to the tugboat captain's predictions, once the *Gunilda* was freed, she listed starboard and quickly sank. Within minutes, she plunged 280 feet to Lake Superior's rocky bottom. Unable to retrieve the boat from those depths, the Harkness party boarded a train to New York

The Gunilda *sinking in Lake Superior* **WikiCommons**

and filed a claim for the boat with insurer Lloyd's of London. That may have ended the story of the yacht for the boat's owner, but the sinking launched a second life for the famous vessel.

Divers spent decades searching for the elusive ship, largely because of the rumors that started as soon as she plunged below the surface. It was thought that a fortune went down with the ship and was waiting for the diver brave enough to reach it. Treasure hunters believed the rumors that the sunken ship held hidden riches, with some saying she held "$300,000 in English china and silver, $500,000 in money and jewels, and cases of rare wines and liquors." For years divers flocked to the spot, hoping to find the *Gunilda*, and some died in the quest to reach the famed yacht.

In 1967, a diver briefly reached the wreck for the first time, a feat that was duplicated in the 1970s, but these dives were short and dangerous endeavors that did not reveal much about the condition of the boat. As diving technology improved, it became possible to reach its depths and explore what remained of the *Gunilda*. In 1980, The Cousteau Society used the *Calypso* to locate and photograph the wreck. The images revealed a remarkably well-preserved ship that suffered no damage during its sinking. The dark, cold water protected the vessel from deterioration so well that the ship's bell still gleamed and its wood retained its paint. Now thought to be among the most beautiful and well-preserved wrecks on the Great Lakes, the ship draws skilled technical divers from all over the world who long to explore this relic of the Gilded Age.

A BLIZZARD'S ICY EMBRACE: SS *KAMLOOPS* (1924–1927)

Something in the snow caught the eye of fur trapper Louis Coutu as he walked along the mouth of the Agawa River in December of 1928. Taking a closer look, he noticed the glittering object reflecting sunlight was a bottle. Curious, he picked up the bottle and saw there was something inside. Carefully opening the bottle, he shimmied the tightly coiled paper from the glass and unrolled it. Squinting at the barely legible script, he scanned the page and realized he found something that would solve a yearlong mystery and just might make him rich.

The mystery of the *Kamloops* began sometime in the evening of December 6, 1927. The 250-foot iron cargo ship was spotted by the SS *Quedoc* in the distance along the rocky shoals of Isle Royale while both ships were battling a tremendous storm on Lake Superior. Thirty-foot waves were pounding the vessels as arctic winds howled in from the north. With temperatures at minus-20 degrees Fahrenheit, the thick layer of ice forming on the boat was growing with each drenching wave that washed over it. The ice weighted the *Kamloops* down, causing her embattled engines to work even harder to propel the ship through the storm. The raging blizzard, coupled with the heavy frost

The lake freighter SS Kamloops *sailing the Lakes* **Lake Erie's Yesterdays OhioLINK Digital Resource Commons**

fog, made visual navigation impossible through the dangerous shoals. The ship blindly pressed forward, towards the shelter of Thunder Bay. The *Quedoc* signaled the *Kamloops* that she was dangerously near the ship-destroying shoals, but her warnings may have been lost in the roar of the storm. Then, blinded by the swirling snow, the *Quedoc* lost sight of the *Kamloops*. That was the last time she, and the twenty-two souls aboard, were ever seen.

Efforts were made to look for the missing ship, but the weather made the task difficult. The storm that pounded the missing ship raged on for days, reaching her zenith on December 12. The Coast Guard cutters that went in search of the boat battled gale-force winds, sub-freezing temperatures, and damage to their ships. The search, which put the lives of the rescuers in jeopardy, was determined too dangerous to continue. The crew was presumed dead, but there remained a hope the boat ran aground and was iced in for the season. Calculations were made that determined, with careful use, the *Kamloops* had enough fuel and provisions to make it through winter. During those bitter months, lighthouse keepers in northern Superior were instructed to keep a watchful eye for the boat. The search for the missing ship recommenced in the spring of 1928. The Coast Guard resumed their water search, and the *Kamloops* owners hired a plane to search for the boat from the air, but she could not be found. In May, fishermen found two bodies washed up on Isle Royale and a scattering of wreckage that was thought to be from the *Kamloops*. Days later, six more bodies were discovered, but the cargo ship remained elusive.

It was what Coutu discovered at the close of that year that helped to shed light on what happened to the *Kamloops*. The message in a bottle was from Alice Bettridge, one of the two women who worked in the ship's kitchen. Discovered 150 miles from where it was thought the boat sank, the note stated:

> I am the last one left alive, freezing and starving to death on Isle Royale in Lake Superior. I just want my mom and dad to know my fate.
> Al(ice), who is dead

The trapper held the key to the mystery of what happened to the *Kamloops*, and he figured someone would be willing to pay for the information. He let it be known that he found a letter from the missing ship but would not reveal its contents or who wrote the letter and that he would turn over the letter to the highest bidder. This mercenary tactic was met with outrage, and soon the validity of the yet unseen letter was called into question. Before the close of January 1929, the letter was released, and the handwriting of the letter was verified by Bettridge's parents. The letter meant that, despite battling gale-force winds and temperatures of minus-30 degrees Fahrenheit, somehow members of the *Kamloops* crew managed to reach shore. How long they were able to remain alive in those conditions will never be known. For fifty years, Bettridge's message to her parents remained the final word on the whereabouts of the *Kamloops*.

In 1977, a group of divers discovered the ship that had been missing for half a century. Based on their exploration of the wreckage, they managed to piece together the terrible final hours on the *Kamloops*. The wreck, found 240 feet below the surface, was so beautifully preserved by the dark, frigid water the divers could clearly observe that the last telegraph sent from the ship indicated that the ship's engines had failed. It appears that she dropped her anchors to avoid being blown into the nearby rocky shoals, but the ship could not hold her location in the brutal storm. The heavy ice that rapidly formed on the ship caused it to list to starboard. By this point, it has been surmised that the boat lost power, so the crew aboard battled against the storm in the dark and without heat to protect them from the arctic temperatures that continued to plunge, reaching as low as minus-30 degrees Fahrenheit that night.

The ship was then jammed to the port side with a force that was certain to have knocked the crew from their feet, as the ship crashed into the rocks they had been working tirelessly to avoid. The wind ground the side of the ship into the jagged stone, and the captain, with the knowledge that the ship could not be saved, called for the crew to lower the one wooden lifeboat available on the *Kamloops* into the crashing waves. In the darkness, it is not known how many of the crew were able to successfully jump from the deck of the *Kamloops* into the small boat or how many miscalculated her location and leapt into the icy waters and disappeared under the waves. Some crew stayed with the captain aboard the ship, hoping the vessel would beach itself on the rocks. Instead, the ship was torn open by the waves, filled with water, and quickly plunged to the bottom of the lake.

While exploring the wreck, divers discovered it wasn't just the ship that the lake had preserved; there was also at least one crew member still aboard the sunken vessel. Temperatures hover just a few degrees above freezing at the bottom of Superior, creating conditions that mimic an ice-water mummification process. The frigid waters, coupled with the lack of sunlight, make the bottom of the lake a difficult environment for the bacteria that cause decomposition to live. Divers have made this lost sailor famous, dubbing him Grampa, Ole Whitey, and sometimes Grampa Whitey. The alabaster-white corpse, still wearing his wedding ring, remains in the ship's engine room. Legends swirl around this startlingly well-preserved corpse who can be seen moving in the boat. Some claim it is the currents in the water that animate the body, while others are certain there are supernatural forces that move the body in an effort to communicate with divers. The well-known lost sailor remains in his ice-water grave to this day.

Ultimately, only nine of the twenty-two people aboard the *Kamloops* when it went down were ever recovered. Five of the bodies were claimed by their families and taken home for their final rest. Four of the bodies were never identified and were buried in an unmarked grave at the Riverside Cemetery in Thunder Bay. Canadian Steamship Lines, the company which owned the *Kamloops*, paid for the burial of the four bodies, and promised to erect a stone memorial in their honor when they were interred in 1928. In 2011, with the help of the Thunder Bay Museum, the men finally received a monument to mark their final resting place. The thirteen bodies that were never recovered, like the boat itself, remain somewhere in Lake Superior's icy depths.

COX'S UNLUCKY YEAR: SS *GEORGE M. COX* (1901–1933)

The year 1933 was a terrible time for New Orleans businessman and multimillionaire George M. Cox. Looking at his string of bad luck that year, the least of the events may have been the sinking of his eponymously named boat on May 27, 1933.

The *George M. Cox* was originally named the *Puritan* when she was launched in 1901. The 307-foot-long former Navy vessel was converted into what was described as a "floating palace" by the Cox-owned Duke Transportation Company. Cox planned to turn the ship into an elegant passenger ship that would make four-day runs between Chicago, Mackinac Island, and the Georgian Bay. The luxurious vessel set sail from Chicago on May 24 with thirty-two elite passengers chosen by Cox to join the maiden voyage. The boat was bound for Port Arthur and would return to Chicago with two hundred and fifty Canadians who were scheduled to attend the 1933 World's Fair held in the Windy City.

The steamer enjoyed easy seas on the journey, and by Saturday, May 27, the ship reached the notorious shoals of Isle Royale. The area, studded with jagged stones, was often enshrouded in fog, making the dangerous area even more challenging to sail through. It was around five in the evening when the ship, traveling at 17 knots (19.5 mph) through the dense fog, began to skirt the shoals. The nearby Rock of

The George M. Cox *sinking in Lake Superior*   **Lake Erie's Yesterdays OhioLINK Digital Resource Commons**

Ages lighthouse, positioned on a rocky outcropping in the shoals, could see the top of the ship as she neared the dangerous reef. Keeper John Soldenski sounded the fog siren to alert the vessel of the impending danger, but the ship continued on without slowing. Many of the passengers were enjoying their evening meal in the dining room when they heard the mournful sound of the foghorn call across the water. Within moments, all aboard felt a violent jolt. The *Cox* struck a rock with such force that the ship's engine and boilers were torn loose.

The impact threw passengers to the floor and caused tables and chairs to soar across the decks. As those aboard scrambled to get their bearings, the ship listed to ninety degrees. The hold quickly filled with water. In just four minutes after the collision, the ship's stern was submerged. Soon, only the top deck would remain above water. An SOS alert was sent over the ship's wireless, and lifesaving measures began. The crew acted quickly, lowering the lifeboats and filling the first two wooden ships with the women and children aboard. One eleven-year-old boy was heard comforting his mother, telling her not to cry as he was having a wonderful time. Within forty-five minutes, the ship had been fully evacuated.

Despite the intensity of the collision, there were few injuries that resulted from the accident. A stewardess with a wrenched back, a battered deckhand, and a cook burned by hot grease were the only ones who were hurt severely enough to need medical attention. These crew, along with a nurse and boat owner Cox, were quickly taken to the mainland by the nearby *Morris B Tremaine*, who responded to the ship's call for assistance. The remaining 118 people made their way to the Rock of Ages to seek shelter.

The rocky outcropping upon which the lighthouse is built is scarcely larger than the lighthouse itself. With nothing but Superior's cold waves around them, the passengers and crew spent an uncomfortable night in the shoal, waiting to be rescued. The thirty-two passengers from Chicago lost their luggage and all personal effects on the ship. They fled with only what they were wearing, and for most, it was inadequate for the cold and damp night air. The lightkeeper's wife kept hot coffee brewing throughout the night, and the spiral staircase was filled with castaways seeking shelter from the cold. The building was far too small to house everyone, so the shivering crew rotated between the lighthouse and the outdoors until the Coast Guard cutter, *Crawford*, arrived on Sunday to transport the group to the nearby city of Houghton. Despite the ordeal, there was not a single casualty in this accident, other than the ship itself. Unsalvageable and abandoned on the shoals, she would later be broken up by powerful autumn storms and sink to the bottom of Lake Superior's icy depths.

A later inquest would determine First Mate Arthur Kronk was responsible for the collision. The *Cox* was led by Captain George E. Johnson on that journey. The captain sailed the area often and knew of the dangers that lurked in the shallow shoals. He designed a route that avoided the treacherous area. Kronk assumed Johnson's duties while the captain was in his stateroom and changed the course of the ship without the captain's knowledge or authorization. Supported by the testimony of the wheelman and other members of the crew, Kronk was determined to be at fault for the sinking of the ship.

For the remainder of the year, trouble continued to follow Cox. His second boat, the lake steamer *Isle Royale*, made headlines in the fall of that year when the crew attempted a mutiny. The ship was docked in Chicago, and Cox was in his stateroom when the sailors held the ship for non-payment. Claiming Cox owed them $18,000 in back pay, the crew seized the ship. Three squads of Chicago police officers arrived to thwart the uprising, but that was not the last time Cox would tangle with *Isle Royale* sailors.

After five weeks in Chicago, Cox returned to his Lake Pontchartrain home to discover his twenty-seven-year-old wife, Thelma, two-year-old son, George Jr., and his in-laws were missing from the estate. Cox noted that also missing from the home were $10,000 in jewels and $9,000 from their joint bank account. After discovering the house empty, Cox received strange telephone calls demanding $25,000 for the return of his family. The calls, which originated from Chicago, claimed the family members were safe, and they would remain safe if he paid the ransom demanded. Believing his family to have been kidnapped, he called the authorities, and before the day had ended, the alleged kidnapping was national news.

It was soon discovered that the family had not been kidnapped but rather left on their own accord. The group had been in Chicago to gather evidence of Cox's infidelity. When Thelma Cox filed for divorce on the grounds of infidelity, she specifically named two Chicago women in the suit. An embarrassed Cox commented to the media that he was confused by the strange events of the previous days, but he was also relieved that his family was safe. The week following the presumed kidnapping, the pair faced each other in court.

Thelma, who was Cox's second wife, had been his secretary for eight years before they married in 1930 and knew how to access family money. When Cox was called into court to begin paying spousal support during their divorce proceedings, he claimed that while he was worth in excess of two million dollars, his wife had seized all of his stock, bonds, and cash from his personal holding company, leaving him with only the $10 in liquid assets that a friend had lent him before his

The George M Cox *continues to slip under Superior's cold water.*   **Lake Erie's Yesterdays OhioLINK Digital Resource Commons**

court date. Mrs. Cox acknowledged she did take the assets in question and requested the court award her $5,000 per month to support herself and her son during the divorce proceedings. After cross-examination, she admitted she could live on a monthly allowance of $1,000, which the court awarded to her.

In another strange turn of events, the telephone call requesting money for the return of his family was placed by William Davis Jr., who worked for Cox on the *Isle Royale.* The twenty-seven-year-old sailor was arrested by the FBI a day after the ransom call had been placed.

After a year where Cox's boat was both the first shipwreck of the season and, at $200,000, the biggest financial loss of the season, and followed by an attempted mutiny, a public scandal, and an expensive divorce, Cox ended the year being sued by his lawyer, J. Studebaker Lucas, for $43,774.76 in unpaid legal fees. For George Cox, 1933 was definitely a very bad year.

THE WRATH OF THE NOVEMBER WITCH: SS *EDMUND FITZGERALD* (1958–1975)

As the weather turns colder, the Great Lakes become more deadly. Gales, sustained surface winds measured between 34 to 47 knots (1 knot is the equivalent of 1.15078 miles per hour), can occur at any time of the year, but the November Gales have a reputation for their particularly perilous force. When joined by the destructive November Witch, strong winds that howl across the Great Lakes that are created by the mixing of arctic air from Canada and warm air from the south, there is no safety on the open water. Formed when air masses collide over the Lakes, they create hurricane-force winds. For sustained winds to be categorized as being of hurricane force, they must move at a minimum of 74 miles per hour. The Witch made her appearance on November 10, 1975, as the *Edmund Fitzgerald* was en route to Detroit. She roared along the water at a sustained speed of 67 miles per hour, with frequent wind gusts of up to 86 miles per hour. The wind whipped the water into thirty-five-foot waves. The November Witch stirred the lake like it was her cauldron, and the ships caught in her path had few options.

The Edmund Fitzgerald *Greenmars Creative Commons CC BY-SA 3.0*

It was during that brutal November storm that the *Edmund Fitzgerald* disappeared, catapulting the massive freighter into the lore of the Great Lakes. As one of the most famous wrecks on the chain of Lakes, her legend endures, in part, because of the mysterious way she disappeared beneath the waves that fateful day.

An Inauspicious Start

There are some who believe the fate of the mighty freighter was sealed long before she set sail from Superior, Wisconsin, on November 9, 1975. Completed in 1956, she was the longest and most expensive boat ever to sail the waterways, with a price tag of $8 million and a length of 729 feet, which exceeds the length of two football fields. Named *Edmund Fitzgerald* in honor of the chairman of Northwestern Mutual, the boat's owner, she broke speed and load-carrying records while she sailed the Lakes.

Nearly 15,000 observers came to the boat's first public showing to witness her christening. The modern tradition of smashing a bottle of champagne on the bow of a newly launched ship has origins in ancient rites. Over five thousand years ago, the Babylonians recorded the sacrifice of an oxen to appease the gods and ensure safe passage for the new ship and her crew. Greek and Roman cultures also had rituals surrounding the launch of new ships. Other cultures used wine, prayer, holy relics, and a host of other techniques to protect the ship and secure its good fortune. The *Edmund Fitzgerald's* christening was not a success. Fitzgerald's wife, Elizabeth, was to christen the boat with a bottle of champagne. Firmly clutching the neck of the bottle in her hand, she struck the glass bottle against the bow of the ship, but the bottle did not break. She tried again a second time, this time putting more force into her swing, yet when the bottle made contact with the bow again, it still did not break. On her third try, the glass shattered, finally completing the ritual. It is thought to be bad luck if the first attempt at shattering the bottle on the bow fails. Mariners are a famously superstitious group, and the failed christening did not go unnoticed by those who put stock in omens.

Moments later, the boat was eased into the water, but the crew experienced problems releasing the keel from its blocks, which resulted in the ship jerking its way into the water. The ship's tumble into the lake created a powerful wave that drenched many of those gathered to honor the launch of the freighter. Now in the water and rocking wildly, the ship washed back and crashed against the dock. The event was so shocking that a water-soaked onlooker experienced a heart attack while on the observation deck and died soon after. This unexpected death, coupled with the difficult christening, was enough for the superstitious to believe the events at the boat's launch foreshadowed its future tragedy.

The Final Run

The winds were light and the weather mild when the freighter left the Burlington Northern Railroad Dock No. 1, in Superior, Wisconsin, loaded with 26,000 tons of iron on November 9, 1975, at 2:20 in the afternoon. On board were twenty-nine men, led by Captain Ernest

McSorely. The respected leader was on his very final run before his retirement after working the waterways for more than forty years.

The journey began as an uneventful one until, without warning, the winds on the lake shifted, bringing an arctic blast into the area. The ship pressed on, and the storm grew. Before long, the boat was battling fifteen-foot waves and wind gusts that topped 50 miles per hour. Snow and spray obscured the men's vision, and the ship was pounded by the relentless winds and waves, which soon began to take on water and list to one side.

McSorely assessed the situation, and by 3:30 that afternoon, he knew the boat was in trouble and in need of aid. He was running both of the *Fitzgerald*'s pumps in an attempt to manage the water pouring into the boat. The captain radioed a nearby ship, the *Arthur Anderson*, saying:

> *Anderson*, this is the *Fitzgerald*. I have sustained some topside damage. I have a fence rail down, two vents lost or damaged, and a list. . . . Will you stay by me 'til I get to Whitefish?

Captain Cooper of the *Anderson* agreed to stay near the ailing ship until she reached the safety of Whitefish Point, Michigan.

At four that afternoon, McSorely radioed the *Anderson* again, stating, "I have lost both radars. Can you provide me with radar plots until we reach Whitefish Bay?" The *Anderson* agreed to keep the *Fitzgerald* advised on her position.

The storm continued to rage, with waves between eighteen and twenty-five feet high pummeling the ship, and the wind gusts topped 80 miles per hour. On board, circumstances continued to grow worse on the failing ship. At six that evening, McSorley radioed another nearby ship, the *Avafors*, stating, "I have a bad list, lost both radars. And am taking heavy seas over the deck. One of the worst seas I've ever been in."

The embattled ship received a message from the *Anderson* at seven that evening, informing the captain the ship was only fifteen miles away from land. Ten minutes later, the *Anderson* again radioed to tell the *Fitzgerald* she had only nine miles until she reached safety. McSorely

Edmund Fitzgerald *Lifeboat No. 2 recovered from the wreck* **shipwrecklog.com is licensed under CC BY-ND 2.0**

radioed back, saying they were holding their own and was relieved to hit land soon. The conversation was the last anyone would ever have with the men aboard the *Fitzgerald*.

Moments later, the *Edmund Fitzgerald* disappeared from the *Arthur Anderson*'s radar screen. The concerned sailors immediately radioed the battered ship but received no response. At 7:39 in the evening, the *Anderson* radioed the emergency Coast Guard line, reporting they lost the boat on their radar. Not only was the ship gone from their radar, but they could not see any lights on the water where the ship had been and could get no radio response from the disabled ship.

A night search on the stormy lake began, but it was fruitless. All that could be found that night were two splintered lifeboats from the freighter and a single, unoccupied life jacket. A search for the *Edmund Fitzgerald* continued for a week, until a rescue boat utilizing a sonar device discovered the wreckage of the great ship at the bottom of icy Lake Superior, 530 feet below the water's surface. The ship's steel hull had been ripped into two pieces, the bow section was upright, and the stern section was upside down. About two hundred feet of the ship's midsection had been obliterated. All twenty-nine souls on the ship that night went down with her. It had happened so suddenly that no call for help was placed from the boat.

What happened between 7:10 in the evening when the ship made its last radio contact and 7:39 when it disappeared without a trace remains a mystery. The suddenness of the ships sinking still shocks people today. What could have happened that was so sudden that there was no time to radio for help or for the men to deploy lifeboats? How had the great boat gone down so quickly that a nearby boat caught no sight of it?

Today, the *Fitzgerald*'s remains lie on the Canadian side of the lake. The location of the wreckage is the gravesite of the twenty-nine men lost and is legally protected from unregulated divers. It is likely we will never learn what happened during the ship's final moments before she plunged into the murky deep, where she remains. Today we still remember this legendary ship and the sons, husbands, and fathers who were lost on that November day. In July of 1995, at the wishes of the family members of those lost in the wreck, the bell of the *Edmund Fitzgerald* was cut from her bow, raised from the frigid waters, and placed on display at the Great Lakes Shipwreck Museum in Sault Ste Marie, Michigan. Each November 10, the bell is tolled thirty times, twenty-nine times for each of the men lost on the *Fitzgerald* and a final toll for the estimated thirty-thousand other souls who have lost their lives in maritime disasters on the Great Lakes.

The Song that Turned the Ship into a Legend

The legend of the *Edmund Fitzgerald* endures, in part, because this modern tragedy was immortalized in song by Canadian singer-songwriter Gordon Lightfoot. "The Wreck of the *Edmund Fitzgerald*," released in 1976, a haunting song without a chorus and a playtime of nearly six minutes, was an unlikely pop radio hit, but its popularity could not be denied. Based on the melody from an Irish folk song, the tune was nominated for two Grammys and made it to number two on the *Billboard* Hot 100 music charts in the United States, while it topped the charts in Canada. The lyrics were written after Lightfoot read an account of the sinking published by *Newsweek* two weeks after that fateful night of November 10, 1975. Over the years, the musician has tweaked the lyrics slightly to both correct a few factual errors in the original lyrics and to acknowledge new information uncovered as investigators continued to learn more about the tragedy.

BIBLIOGRAPHY

"118 die aboard cruise ship SS Noronic." Morningside. Canadian Broadcasting Corporation. August 18, 1977. CBC Digital Archives. cbc.ca/archives/entry/1949-118-die-aboard-cruise-ship-ss-noronic.

"118 Escape As Vessel Hits Reef in Lake." *The Times*. Shreveport, Louisiana, May 29, 1933.

Ali Childs, Arcynta. "A Michigan Museum of Shipwrecks." *Smithsonian Magazine*, April 20, 2011. smithsonianmag.com/travel/a-michigan-museum-of-shipwrecks-2152249/.

Ashcroft, Brent. "Le Griffon: The Great Lakes' greatest mystery." *Detroit Free Press*. February 13, 2015. freep.com/story/news/local/michigan/2015/02/13/le-griffon-shipwreck-great-lakes/23344219/.

Ashlee, Laura R. "Broken in Two." *Michigan History Magazine*. November/December 1990.

Balfour, David. "The Actions of H.P. BOPE, L.C.HANNA, J.G. MUNRO and the Tragedy of the CLARION on December 8, 1909." Inland Seas Online. National Museum of the Great Lakes, Fall 2014. nmgl.org/the-actions-of-the-h-p-bope-l-c-hanna-j-g-munro-and-the-tragedy-of-the-clarion-on-december-8-1909-fall-2014/.

Bourrie, Mark. *Many a Midnight Ship: True Stories of Great Lakes Shipwrecks*. Ann Arbor, MI: University of Michigan Press, 2005.

Bowen, Curt. "Wreck of the Kamloops." *Advanced Diver Magazine*. January 2006.

Boyer, Dwight. *Ghost Ships of the Great Lakes*. Cleveland, OH: Cleveland Freshwater Press, Inc., 1968.

"Burns to the Water's Edge." *The Marion Star*. Marion, OH. December 9, 1909.

Butts, Edward. *Shipwrecks, Monsters and Disasters of the Great Lakes*. Toronto: Tundra Books, 2010.

"Captain Insists Course Changed." *Lansing State Journal*. May 31, 1933.

Carper, Shelby. "200-Year-Old Shipwreck Discovered At Bottom Of Lake Ontario." *Forbes*. August 18, 2016. Retrieved August 27, 2020. forbes.com/sites/shelbycarpenter/2016/08/18/200-year-old -shipwreck-found-bottom-lake-ontario/#2410b2f348d9.

Carter, Jim. "Strange dream, tragedy along Superior's Graveyard Coast." *The Mining Journal*. Marquette, MI. April 26, 2017.

Chicago Stories. "The Eastland Disaster." John Callaway. WTTW Chicago PBS. Original airdate July 20, 2018.

"Clarion's Survivors." *Buffalo Evening News*. December 10, 1909.

"Coal Laden Vessel Sinks." *Buffalo Evening News*. August 9, 1917.

"Coast Guards Search Lake for Steamer." *The Windsor Star*. Windsor, Ontario, Canada. December 14, 1927.

"Death of Old Captain Revives Yarn." *Democrat and Chronicle*. Rochester, NY. April 10, 1927.

Donahue, James. *Terrifying Steamboat Stories*. Bloomfield, MI: Altwerger & Mandel Publishing Co. Inc., 1991.

"Eleven Hunt in Unparalleled Summer Storm." *The Indiana Gazette*. Indiana, PA. June 27, 1930.

"From Lake to New Life." *Kansas City Times*. March 8, 1927.

Godfrey, Linda. *Weird Michigan: Your Travel Guide to Michigan's Local Legends and Best Kept Secrets*. New York: Sterling, 2006.

Gowen, Rob. "Plaque to honour SS Asia survivor." *Owen Sound Sun Times*. October 17, 2018.

Gmiter, Tanda. "Mystery surrounds old Lake Michigan shipwreck, woman left tied to mast." *Michigan Live*. Updated January 29, 2019. Retrieved October 10, 2020. mlive.com/entertainment/ 2018/10/mystery_surrounds_old_lake_mic.html.

Haddad, Ken. "The Bermuda Triangle of the Great Lakes: The Lake Michigan Triangle." WDIV/ClickOnDetroit.com. April 28, 2018. clickondetroit.com/all-about-michigan/2018/04/29/the-bermuda -triangle-of-the-great-lakes-the-lake-michigan-triangle/.

Hale, Dennis N. *Shipwrecked: Reflections of the Sole Survivor*. Self-published, 2010.

"Harkness Yacht Ashore." *New York Tribune*. August 31, 1911.

Hauch, Valerie. "Once Upon a City: The Day the SS Noronic Turned Toronto's Waterfront into a Deadly Inferno." Thestar.com, *Toronto Star*. September 17, 2015. thestar.com/yourtoronto/once-upon -a-city-archives/2015/09/17/once-upon-a-city-the-day-the-ss -noronic-turned-torontos-waterfront-into-a-deadly-inferno.html.

"Hearts Bowed Down." *The Sandusky Register*. Sandusky, OH. September 7, 1892.

Johnston, Laura. "The Myth of Bessie, the Lake Erie Monster: Remember When." *Rock the Lake*. Cleveland Lakefront Collaborative. December 27, 2017. Retrieved September 3, 2020. rockthelake .com/buzz/2017/12/myth-bessie-lake-erie-monster/.

Kadar, Wayne Louis. *Great Lakes Passenger Ship Disasters*. Gwinn, MI: Avery Color Studios, Inc., 2005.

Kates, William. "Explorers Find 1780 British Warship in Lake Ontario." Yahoo! News, Associated Press. June 13, 2008. web .archive.org/web/20080614182044/news.yahoo.com/s/ap/ 20080613/ap_on_sc/shipwreck_found.

Kennard, Jim. "Shipwreck Explorers Discover HMS Ontario - 1780 British Warship in Lake Ontario." *Shipwreck World*. June 13, 2018. shipwreckworld.com/articles/shipwreck-explorers-discover-1780 -british-warship-in-lake-ontario.

Kohl, Cris, and Joan Forsberg. *Shipwrecks at Death's Door*. Chicago: Seawolf Communications, 2007.

Lardinois, Anna. *Milwaukee Ghosts and Legends*. Charleston, SC: History Press, 2018.

Lardinois, Anna. *Storied & Scandalous Wisconsin*. Guilford, CT: Globe Pequot Press Inc., 2020.

Lewis, Walter. "Atlantic (Steamboat), Sunk by Collision, 20 Aug 1852." Maritime History of the Great Lakes, Our Digital World. images .maritimehistoryofthegreatlakes.ca/details.asp?ID=39249.

"Lightning Hits Boat at Brockville, Killing 30." *The Ottawa Evening Journal*. Ottawa, Ontario, Canada. June 27, 1930.

"Lone Survivor Always Afraid of Storms." *The Ithaca Journal*. December 1, 1966.

Long, Megan. *Ghosts of the Great Lakes More than Mere Legend*. Holt, MI: Thunder Bay Press, 2003.

Lundmark, Jodi. "Stone now marks burial plot for SS Kamloops tragedy." *Thunder Bay Newswatch*. Dougall Media. December 9, 2011. tbnewswatch.com/local-news/stone-now-marks-burial-plot-for-ss -kamloops-tragedy-389568.

Maki, Allen. "The lady in the lake and the man who must have her." *Maclean's*. August 22, 1977.

"Marooned in Lake Superior." *The Burlington Free Press*. September 1, 1911.

Martin, Jay C. "The Advocates Devil: The Maritime Public Historian as Expert Witness." *The Public Historian* 37, no. 1 (February 2015): 25–38.

Mazet, Horace S. "Australian Bushrangers and Convict Ships." *The Military Engineer* 24, no. 137 (1932): 509–13. Accessed August 17, 2020. jstor.org/stable/44566412.

Metzger, Patrick. "Toronto Urban Legends: The Great Serpent of Lake Ontario." *Torontoist*. January 16, 2013. Retrieved September 10, 2020. torontoist.com/2013/01/toronto-urban-legends-the-great -serpent-of-lake-ontario/.

Oleszewski, Wes. *Great Lakes Ghost Stories Haunted Tales Past & Present*. Gwinn, MI: Avery Color Studios, 2004.

Palmer, Richard. "On the Waterfront: The Legendary Lake Ontario sea serpent." *Oswego County News Now*. May 16, 2020. Retrieved September 10, 2020. oswegocountynewsnow.com/columnists/on -the-waterfront-the-legendary-lake-ontario-sea-serpent/article_6d 14c2c2-977a-11ea-9315-db5e3e26e8d8.html.

Ratigan, William. *Great Lakes Shipwrecks and Survivals*. Grand Rapids, MI: William B. Eerdmans Publishing Company, 1977.

Reilly, III, F. Kent, et al. *Ancient Objects and Sacred Realms*. Austin, TX: University of Texas Press, 2010.

Schumacher, Michael. *Wreck of the Carl D. A True Story of Loss, Survival and Rescue at Sea*. Beverly, MA: Quarry Books, 2010.

"A shipwreck, a young woman and a message in a bottle." *Soo Today.* May 26, 2019. Retrieved August 3, 2020. sootoday.com/columns/ remember-this/a-shipwreck-a-young-woman-and-a-message-in -a-bottle-1473946.

Sinclair, Andy. "Final Mission." *Lake Magazine.* Small Newspaper Group. November 2008.

Soini, Paul D. "Hale Tells of Ship Sinking." *The Times Herald.* Port Huron, MI. December 2, 1966.

Steere, Mike. "Superior keeps its shipwrecks fresh Preservation: In the cold, almost sterile water at the bottom of the Great Lake, divers find the remains of marine disasters." *The Baltimore Sun.* May 12, 1996.

Stonehouse, Frederick. *Haunted Lake Michigan.* Duluth, MN: Lake Superior Port Cities, Inc., 2006.

Stonehouse, Frederick. "Lights of Michigan's Shipwreck Coast: Beacons on the Lonely Shore." *Lake Superior Magazine*, September 1, 2003. lakesuperior.com/the-lake/maritime/lights-of-michigans -shipwreck-coast-beacons-on-the-lonely-shore/.

Talbott, Linda. "Twelve Worst Maritime Disasters in Great Lake History." 2012. U.S. Data Repository. us-data.org/mi/glm/shipwrecks/ g-p-griffith.txt.

"Terrible Marine Disaster." *The York Dispatch.* September 18, 1882.

"Thirty-One Men Lost in Explosion." *Olean Evening Times.* June 27, 1930.

Thompson, Mark L. *Graveyard of the Lakes.* Detroit, MI: Wayne State University Press, 2004.

"Thursday, September 14 marks the 135th Anniversary of the loss of the Asia." *Manitoulin Expositor.* September 13, 2017.

"Twenty Six Perish." *Chicago Tribune.* September 2, 1892.

United States Department of Interior, National Park Service. "Isle Royale." National Park Michigan. Retrieved August 1, 2020. nps .gov/isro/index.htm.

Varhola, Michael J. *Shipwrecks and Lost Treasures: Great Lakes, Legends and Lore, Pirates and More!* Guilford, CT: The Globe Pequot Press, 2008.

"Video of Wreck Reveals Eerie Underwater Tomb." *The Windsor Star.* October 8, 1992.

Vogel, Mike, et al. "Treasure Ship Discovered in Lake Erie, Divers Say." *The Buffalo News.* June 26, 1991.

Vyhnak, Carola. "One man's quest to recover artifacts from Lake Ontario shipwreck brings little-known part of Canada's heritage to light." *The Star.* August 18, 2012. Retrieved August 26, 2020. thestar.com/news/canada/2012/08/18/one_mans_quest_to_recover_artifacts_from_lake_ontario_shipwreck_brings_little-known_part_of_canadas_heritage_to_light.html.

Wangemann, Bill. "Bannockburn one of the Ghost Ships of the Great Lakes." *The Sheboygan Press.* April 19, 2005.

Wheeler, Wayne. "Rock of Ages Light Station." *The Keeper's Log.* U.S. Lighthouse Society. Fall 2005.

"Wife, Son, and Her Parents Missing." *The Town Talk.* Alexandria, LA. September 30, 1933.

Winnetka Story: History of Winnetka & Chicago's North Shore. DVD, directed by John Newcombe. Winnetka, IL: Winnetka Historical Society, 2010.

Worrell, Chris M. "Author discusses deadly 1850 Lake Erie Shipping Disaster." Cleveland.com. January 12, 2019. cleveland.com/euclid/2011/10/author_discusses_deadly_1850_l.html.

GLOSSARY OF NAUTICAL TERMS

A

Aft: When you move towards the back, or stern of the boat, you are moving aft.

Aground: Aground describes a boat that runs ashore or is stuck on the bottom of a lake or other body of water.

Ahead: When the boat is moving in a forward direction

Alee: Facing away from the wind

Amidship: The central or middle part of the vessel

Astern: When the boat is moving in a backward or reverse direction

Avast: To stop or to cease

B

Boom: The boom is the horizontal pole that extends from the bottom of the mast. Adjusting the boom towards the direction of the wind is how the sailboat is able to harness wind power in order to move forward or backward.

Bow: Refers to the front end of the boat

Bulkhead: Dividing wall separating compartments on a ship

Buoy: An anchored float used for marking a position on the water

C

Capsize: When a ship or boat lists too far and rolls over in the water, exposing the keel

Course: The direction in which a vessel is being steered, usually given in degrees

D

Deck: The main horizontal parts of a ship's structure
Draught: The depth of a ship's keel below the waterline

F

First Mate: The second-in-command of a commercial ship
Forecastle: A partial deck above the upper deck and at the head of the vessel; often the location of the crew's quarters
Forward: When you move towards the front, or bow of the boat, you are moving forward.
Founder: To fill with water and sink
Freighter: A cargo ship

G

Gangway: An opening in the side of a ship to allow passengers to board or leave the vessel

H

Hatch: An opening in a boat's deck fitted with a watertight cover
Helm: The wheel or tiller controlling the rudder
Hold: A compartment below deck in a large vessel used to carry cargo
Hull: The main body of a vessel
Hurricane Deck: A covered deck on a passenger ship

K

Keel: The centerline of a boat running fore and aft; the backbone of a vessel
Knot: A measure of speed equal to one nautical mile (6,076 feet) per hour

L

Lee: The side of the boat sheltered from the wind

Liner: Any cargo or passenger ship running scheduled service along a specific route with published ports of call

List: A ship's angle of lean or tilt to one side. Typically refers to a lean caused by flooding or improperly loaded or shifted cargo.

M

Mast: A vertical pole on a ship that supports the sails or rigging

Midship: Approximately in the location equally distant from the bow and stern

Mooring: An arrangement for securing a boat to a buoy or a pier

P

Port: Standing at the rear of a boat, facing the bow, the portside of a vessel refers to the entire left side of the boat.

Q

Quarter: The sides of a boat aft of amidships

R

Rigging: A system of ropes, cables, or chains employed to support a ship's masts

Rudder: A vertical plate or board for steering a boat

S

Schooner: A type of boat that has fore-and-aft sails on two or more masts and the forward mast is no taller than the rear masts

Screw: A boat's propeller

Sidewheeler: A paddle steamer propelled by a pair of paddle wheels, one mounted on each side

Starboard: Standing at the rear of a boat, facing the bow, the starboard side of a vessel refers to the entire right side of the boat.

Stem: The forward-most part of the bow

Stern: The stern of a boat is the back portion of the vessel. It is the opposite to the bow of a boat, which is the front.

T

Tiller: A lever used for steering, attached to the top of the rudder
Top side: The part of the hull between the waterline and the deck

U

Up-bound: Traveling against the current

W

Wheel: The steering device on larger vessels; a wheel with a horizontal axis, connected by cables to the rudder
Windward: In the direction that the wind is coming from

Y

Yawl: An un-decked boat, often beach-launched, worked under both oar and sail

INDEX

ABOUT THE AUTHOR

Anna Lardinois, a maritime disaster enthusiast, owns Gothic Milwaukee, Brew City's most popular haunted, historical walking tour company. The creator of *Walking Milwaukee* and the 11th Pfister Narrator, Lardinois loves to celebrate the best Milwaukee has to offer. The author's previous titles include *Milwaukee Ghosts and Legends* and *Storied and Scandalous Wisconsin*.